You Can't See My *Bodyguard*

Trusting in Your Ever-Present God

May you always remember that you never walk alone! Blessings,

LORI QUERIN

Lori Querin

YOU CAN'T SEE MY BODYGUARD

For my parents, Don and Betty Hardister. From as far back as I can remember, you have been faithful to God, to each other, and to your family. The lessons you gave were not through speeches or lectures, but through your actions and selfless deeds. You have taught me the meaning of true religion.

And for my husband and sweetheart, Pete Querin. This book was your idea first, and through your encouragement and belief in me, I was able to stay the course and bring my thoughts to these pages. Thank you, Sweetheart, for building my spirit with words of faith, and challenging me to reach my goals.

Lastly, for my boys, Brandon and Joshua. You impress me with your knowledge, your wisdom, and your strong character. You are my God-given promises and you make this Momma proud.

Acknowledgments

Thank you to:

- my writing coach and friend, Cindi McMenamin, for your guidance, advice, editing, and many words of affirmation and encouragement. The day you said "Lori, you have a book" was the day God brought much-needed confirmation to my spirit about moving forward in writing. Thank you, Cindi, for all the gentle prodding and pushing. That coffee date conversation was a big day for me.

- my brother, Ben. I'm grateful you believe that if a project touches just one person, it's worth it. "It's all pocket change to God" as you say. Your faith has inspired me more times than you know. Thanks for the "pocket change."

- Christina, Cynthia and Nicole, all of the "check-ins" were a little bit like therapy... thanks for the words.

- My mother-in-law, Barbara, and father-in-law, Allen, who gave me the best gift and biggest prize, and who have always been nothing but supportive and kind.

And thank you to my wonderful church family, the people of New Life Ministries in Kingsburg, CA. Together we have climbed mountains of faith and endured treks through the valleys of pain and loss. You are a people who never give up and you have enriched my life with your love. I have been privileged to serve as your P-Lo and I'm grateful for all the wonderful memories and stories I've tucked away. My heart is full of love for you.

Contents

Now to the King eternal, immortal, invisible,
to God who alone is wise, be honor and
glory forever and ever. Amen.

(1 Timothy 1:17)

Unseen but Always There

Wouldn't it be nice to know that wherever you went, whatever situation you were in, you had someone there alongside you for support? Maybe you have friends who've made the declaration to you, "I've got your back." It's comforting to hear, but the reality is, your friend can't be with you in every situation you face. Even the person who loves you the most can't protect you from *every* battle or hardship life brings. Many of the trials we face are those of an unseen nature[1] and much of the time, it is in the depths of our hearts, where we have to muster our strength.

We gather encouragement, advice, and "war strategies" from those closest to us, and those pep talks can help us. Yet, we can still feel — during the most trying times in our lives — that we are left to forge our way to victory alone.

But, do we *really* fight alone?

Early in the morning about two years ago, I was awakened with a thought that was almost like hearing an audible voice: *You can't see my bodyguard.*

I rolled over and thought, *that's random*, but I was intrigued. I had no idea how much that thought would permeate my mind. It was a whispered truth.

I had never before thought of God as being my *bodyguard*. He is the Creator, He is the Savior, and He is my Father and Friend. But… *bodyguard*? Yet as I recalled intimidating situations in the past, looked at painful situations in my present, and even anticipated uncertain days in my future, I realized the many ways in which God has been — and still is — my Bodyguard. He's the Unseen One who watches over my life. The more I ponder that thought, the more grateful I become — grateful that I have a God who loves me, and who is more powerful than any force on this earth. My Bodyguard has been with me every minute of every day from the time I was born until now.

He's not just *my* Bodyguard, though. If you know Him, through a saving relationship with Jesus, He is *your* unseen Bodyguard, too. He's the One who was thinking of you before you were born (Jeremiah 1:5). He's the One who fashioned all your days (Psalm 139:16) and who knows you better than any best friend ever could. He is the One who gave your life purpose (Ephesians 2:10), and the One who helps you fulfill that purpose. He is ever present, all powerful, and everything you need.

No matter where you are on your journey with God – or possibly your journey to try to make it without Him – this is a book to comfort you or convince you that God is near. It's a reminder of how close He is to you and me – going before us, walking alongside us, and watching our backs.

Over the years, I can recall situations in which He has been there for me, even when I may not have realized it at the time. In this book, I will share some of the lessons I've learned and experiences I have had in the presence of the One I call my Father. He's the One who's been a shield about me (Psalm 3:3), guarding my heart and my mind. He's the One who is continually teaching me of His character and loving me through my times of need. All my life He has gently led me from one step in my faith to the next. And if you've welcomed Him into your life, He is already doing the same for you.

Are you ready to connect with the One who is there for you in every area of your life, too? Then let's walk through the chapters of this book together. I hope you will be inspired by biblical truths in each chapter that remind you of His faithfulness and His ability to control all that you can't. And I pray you will glean nuggets of encouragement for your daily life that you can share with others who need to be reminded they have an unseen Bodyguard, too.

As you read these pages may you gain a deeper love for the One who loves and protects you more than you can imagine...your Creator, your Savior, your Bodyguard.

---

[1] Ephesians 6:12 tells us: "For we do not wrestle against flesh and blood, but against principalities, against powers, against the rulers of the darkness of this age, against spiritual hosts of wickedness in the heavenly places" and thus we want to be prepared!

1

He Makes His Presence Known

I remember the night my Bodyguard first made His presence known. I didn't need rescuing from danger. I wasn't trapped in an overturned car, nor was I on the brink of any life-threatening disaster; I was simply a little girl who happened to be attending a revival service in Northern California.

It was a summer night in the mid 1960s and the revival services at Faith Tabernacle Church were going strong. I don't remember the name of the preacher, but he delivered his message with excitement, fire and passion. (You know, the kind of preaching where the spit is flying and the preacher is gasping for air? Back in the 60s that was the norm for revival services.)

There was a lot of conviction in that little church as the man of God was preaching to a packed house. I was attending the service with my mother, my aunt, some siblings and cousins. I remember feeling like a big kid that night, as all of us kids were sitting in a row by ourselves behind my aunt and mother. *Such independence.* We always sat with my parents in church. So, to be sitting in my own row was a rare privilege.

I was about 7 years old and although I don't remember what the preacher was speaking on that evening, the message penetrated my young heart and I became aware of God's presence in a way I never experienced before. I had a head knowledge of Jesus and God, because I'd been going to church my whole short life. But this was an encounter that was going past my head and into my heart. This was something I'd never felt before, and something I wasn't expecting. Jesus was *calling me.*

At some point during the sermon the atmosphere in the room began to change; I went from feeling like a big kid with the pack, to feeling like I was the only one in the room. It was as though God was whispering my name. I felt compelled to get out of my seat and go to the front of the church where they were praying for people. It didn't matter to me that my siblings and cousins were there watching me make my move, I just remember needing to respond.

It was there at the front of the church that I fell to my knees before God, for the very first time. I had no words, I had no prayer. All I could do was sob. I was in the presence of a Holy God who loved me and was calling me to Himself. As I knelt there on my knees, I felt love, acceptance, desire. Not just my desire for God, but somehow, His desire for *me*. The God of Heaven desired a relationship with *me*. And it was okay that I was not a perfect little girl because He loved me regardless. I wasn't the best or the smartest, I was just a simple country girl. And yet God desired to meet with me. I don't know if my 7-year-old mind understood what being unworthy felt like, but looking back, *unworthy* is a word that describes how I was feeling. *Who was I to deserve God's undivided attention?*

The preacher put his hand on my head and prayed for me as I continued to sob. It was a profound moment in my life. I stayed there for quite some time. I could hear the service going on around me and it didn't matter. It didn't matter to me what people were thinking, or how long I was there. I couldn't move from that meeting place with God. That was my moment of spiritual awakening. That was the night God went from someone I had known in my head to someone who made His home in my heart.

Appearing to the Lowly

That experience was more than 50 years ago and I remember it like it was yesterday. That was the day my unseen Bodyguard introduced Himself to me. The God I knew *of* became the God I *knew*. He'd been in my small world all along, watching over me, and waiting for just the right moment to make Himself known to my heart.

Today I'm amazed that such a powerful God would stoop down low to meet with a little girl in a little country church. I still tear up when I think of that special meeting and the power that it held in my life. By the world's standards I was just a little kid of no great importance. But by God's standard, I was precious and He had a meeting to keep…He had an impact to make on a heart, no matter the size.

Jesus' mother, Mary, sings a beautiful song in the first chapter of the Gospel of Luke that speaks of God's dealings with the lowly and simple. In verse 52, Mary sings, "He has put down the mighty from their thrones and exalted the lowly." The Messiah didn't come from royalty or from a big elaborate palace; He came from a young, virtually unknown woman who was lowly, humble, and willing. Jesus, the King of Glory, would be born in a dirty stable in the tiny town of Bethlehem.

Some might think the God of all creation would be mostly interested in the mighty and strong, people of importance, those who'd have much to offer. But the world's standard of importance is completely different than God's standard. His track record proves He takes great pleasure in showing up when we least expect Him – in the most unlikely places and to the most unlikely people.

God doesn't look at people the way the world does. Everyone, from influential to the simple, is of great importance to Him. When He came to be the Savior, He came for all. Jesus Himself tells us in John 12:47 that he didn't come to judge the world but to save the world. From the greatest to the smallest.

It didn't matter where I came from, He knew that little girl before she was formed in her mother's womb (Psalm 139:15-16). He knew the plans He had for her, and He knew the encounter He'd planned for her that night would be something that she would remember for a lifetime. When doubts would arise, when times would get tough, when she would wonder about her place in the world, she would have the memory tucked away in her heart of a real and personal encounter with the living God. She would remember what the love and acceptance of God felt like, and the experience she had that night would strengthen her, give her confidence, and carry her through some difficult days ahead.

Isn't God so good to come close and make Himself known?

Childlike Faith

In Matthew 18, Jesus' disciples asked Him who was greatest in the kingdom of heaven. Jesus answered their question by calling a child into the middle of their group and began to teach about the importance of *becoming* like a child. His disciples probably weren't expecting Jesus to give the answers He gave. But Jesus was a great teacher and He knew how to get his point across. Who's the greatest? Let's take it a little further…how about who will actually be in heaven? This was Jesus' answer:

"Assuredly, I say to you, unless you are converted and become as little children, you will by no means enter the kingdom of heaven. Therefore, whoever humbles himself as this little child is the greatest in the kingdom of heaven." (verses 3-4)

This seems like such a simple answer: Convert your heart and become as a child. I wonder if the disciples felt like it was another one of those verbal "zingers" that Jesus was famous for. Maybe they were expecting a complicated answer. After all, we are talking about the *greatest* in heaven. Yet, Jesus told them to become like a child. The reality of Jesus' answer, though a simple one, is tough – not tough for a child, but definitely tough for the "big people."

When I was a little girl walking up the aisle to meet Jesus that night, it didn't matter to me who was watching. I wasn't thinking about what it would cost me. I wasn't hesitating for fear of a life change. I just needed to surrender to the call. Children don't think about the what-ifs like adults do. Their minds aren't cluttered with preconceived notions and unbelief, or even concerns about their image. Children simply believe. It's no wonder that Jesus says we must become as little children.

When my first-born son, Brandon, was 5 years old he had a "big kid" moment at an evening church service, similar to the one I had. I let him sit on his own with his friends during church that night. When the Pastor gave the invitation for salvation, Brandon rose to his feet and marched up the aisle. He marched right past me like a soldier on a mission. He didn't even look my way. He went all the way to the front of the church.

Trailing behind him were all the kids who were sitting in the row with him. The sermon wasn't geared toward children, but they understood it. Children simply believe and respond. They have no trouble humbling themselves before God. Brandon's response to God's call wasn't emotional like it was for me. It was a simple matter of making a decision. But it was an encounter nonetheless —a walk of obedience to the call of God at 5 years old! My other son, Josh, also had an encounter like mine; he, too, was young when Jesus called him to an altar of prayer. We were having a nighttime service with a guest speaker when Josh made his move. After church service was over, later in the evening, I remember him coming into my bedroom, sitting on my bed, and talking about what he experienced. Hours after the meeting was over, he was still being affected by the presence of God that night.

What About You?

Maybe you, too, have a vivid memory of when God first made

Himself known to you. Perhaps you were a young child, like I was. Or maybe you were older. Regardless of your age, you are blessed to have such a meaningful memory tucked away. But it's also possible you don't recall a God-encounter when you were young or even older in life. If that's the case, it doesn't mean He hasn't sought you. It doesn't mean God hasn't spoken to your heart. Perhaps, it just means you didn't recognize Him.

In Revelation 3:20 we read Jesus' invitation to each of us: "Behold I stand at the door and knock. If anyone hears My voice and opens the door, I will come in to him and dine with him and he with me." Sometimes the Lord's call is a simple knocking, a gentle whisper from the other side of your heart's door, letting you know there is more to life. His call can be a whisper that says, *You are not alone.* His voice from the other side of the door can simply sound like *I'm calling you to be Mine*, accompanied by a knowing that if you surrender, your life will change for the better.

Jesus' call to open the door and dine is a call to an intimate relationship. To sit at the "table" with Jesus means you have His undivided attention and He has yours. It's a beautiful place to begin a relationship. It's a beautiful place to cultivate a friendship.

I don't know why God showed up in my life the way He did that night in church. Apparently, He knew I needed that special encounter with Him that day. It would prove to be an anchoring place and an experience that would stay with me all my life. There have been several times I have returned to that place where my spiritual anchor was lowered, and it has brought me great comfort each time I have.

I've since had several encounters with God through the decades of my life. Some were quite dramatic and some have been very subtle. *How* He calls us is not as important as learning to listen for Him. The cultural noises that surround us in the 21st Century are loud and can make it challenging for us to hear God's voice. Everything today is fast paced. Technology has captured our attention and interrupted our quiet time. It can be easy to neglect what we need the most – to be still in God's presence. Sometimes it's not a matter of being too busy with life that makes hearing God difficult, it's a matter of not being able to tune in to His frequency amidst all the other noise.

A Call to Action

As a 7-year-old child, I had a choice to make in the church that night. I could stay in my seat or I could respond to the call of God. I don't remember the decision being a struggle, I just remember responding. It was a night of simple surrender and obedience to *move*. It was a move to get out from where I was to a place where He was waiting.

God's initial call on our lives is to *move*. James 4:8 tells us if we draw near to God, He will draw near to us. As we age, those "moves" become more difficult to make. Sometimes, as adults we can make finding God so complicated. Much of the time all we need to do is simply cast off pride and surrender our hearts. We must ignore the voice of resistance that fights against surrender. We must move past the crowd and simply obey and respond, regardless of who might be watching. I wonder how many people would follow you and me if we decided to make a move toward God and march down the aisle of obedience.

I don't know where you are in your walk with God, but I know that He loves you the same way He loves me. You might be like I once was and have a head knowledge of God, but not a heart encounter. Or, maybe it's been a while since you've heard God's voice due to the hectic pace of your life. Remember, God's promise to you today is if you draw near to Him, He will draw near to you.

Jeremiah 31:3 says that God loves us with an everlasting love and with lovingkindness *He draws us*. God doesn't change. His love is timeless. And He is still drawing us to Himself with His lovingkindness!

Do you hear Him whispering your name through the atmosphere?

He really does want to make Himself known. Go ahead and make your move. Whether it's a step to meet God for the first time or a step to get to know Him more intimately, His call is to come and dine.

Making Your Move

Take yourself back to the first time you became aware of the presence of God in your life. Did you make a bold move or did you simply know in your heart that He was there? (Describe your experience in the space below.)

1. Which do *you* think is more difficult – coming to God as a child or coming to Him as an adult?

Why do you hold this opinion?

2. Jesus made coming to Him so easy. Read Matthew 11:28-30. What are some of the promises Jesus gave in this portion of Scripture?

What are the requirements of you in these verses?

3. When you and I remember the beautiful accounts of yesterday, it can help us muster strength for today. How have your experiences with God brought you strength today?

Drawing Closer to Your Bodyguard

Hebrews 13:5 says: "For He himself has said 'I will never leave you or forsake you.'" What a beautiful promise. Not only is God promising that He will never leave us alone, but He is also promising that He will not abandon us. He will stay with us no matter what!

He desires your heart and delights in making Himself known to you. He is more accessible than we can imagine and stands ready to have an up close and personal relationship with you.

Maybe you've never prayed a prayer to enter into a relationship with God or maybe it's been a while since you've prayed. I'll leave you with a simple prayer and I know that if you pray it from your heart, He will hear and answer.

Father in Heaven,
I come to You in the name of Your Son, Jesus Christ. I confess that I've sinned and that I'm far away from You. I know I need Jesus to forgive me for my sins, and so I ask You to please forgive me of all wrongdoing and make me clean. Jesus, I ask You to be my Lord and Savior. I want to know You and I want to live my life according to the Scriptures. Help me to seek You and as I do, I'm believing I will find You according to Your promise in Jeremiah 29:13. Teach me Your ways and help me to live for You. Thank You, God, for loving me. Thank You for not abandoning me and thank You for saving me. Amen.

If you prayed this prayer, I would love to hear from you so I can pray for you as you grow in your relationship with Jesus. (Please see my contact information on page 151 and drop me a line when you're ready.)

2

He Sees You in Obscurity

I've always been intrigued with people in the Bible who lived in obscurity and were later brought to the main stage of God's story. They came out of obscurity to accomplish something bold and daring for God. They were relatively unnoticed people who became some of the greatest men and women who lived.

Merriam Webster's online Dictionary defines obscure as *not easily seen, or relatively unknown, remote, not prominent or famous; also, to conceal or hide by covering, to be remote or secluded.*

Are there men and women in the Bible who come to your mind when you read this definition of obscurity? Maybe people in your own life come to mind. I love how God uses the un-famous, un-prominent and seemingly insignificant people to do great things for Him. Let's take a quick look at just two of the many who are recorded in Scripture.

Not One Greater than John

John the Baptist is considered to be one of the "greats." Luke 1:80 tells us this man "grew and became strong in the deserts til the day of his manifestation to Israel." John was "the prophet of the highest and chosen by God to go before the face of the Lord to prepare His way, to give knowledge of salvation to His people" (verses 76-77). There's not a lot of worldly fanfare in the wilderness. But according to this passage, wilderness living makes you stronger. For John, there was a lot of growing in toughness, which probably led to enduring hardship, and most importantly, growing in the knowledge of God. Sometimes our lives can feel like we're taking a detour in the wilderness. But remember friend, great things can happen in the desert places. Like John was, maybe you are being prepared by God in *your* wilderness. Remember, John "became strong" in the desert.

When his time of obscurity in the wilderness ended, John came on the scene like a firebrand preaching repentance, salvation, and baptism. He didn't shy away from preaching the truth. He stood in the face of King Herod and confronted the king for his adulterous affair with his own brother's wife and John didn't mince words with the religious leaders, either. People came to John from all over to be baptized. He taught them so powerfully that they reasoned in their hearts whether or not he was the Messiah. Luke 3:15-16 says: "Now as the people were in expectation, they reasoned in their hearts about John, whether he was the Christ or not, John answered, saying to all, "I indeed baptize you with water; but One mightier than I is coming, whose sandal strap I am not worthy to loose. He will baptize you with the Holy Spirit and fire."

John was chosen by God to end a 400-year-period of prophetic silence. The day of the Messiah had come. Jesus was coming forth from His own obscurity and His cousin John, was the one to prepare the way.

The Scriptures don't give many particulars about John's childhood except that he leaped in his mother's womb when Mary went to visit his mother, Elizabeth (Luke 1:41). After this pre-born encounter with Jesus, we don't hear from John the Baptist again until he prepares the way for Jesus as an adult. Yet it's obvious that John's years of obscurity prepared him to be the forerunner of the Messiah and one of the greatest men to live. Jesus, Himself, said in Matthew 11:11: "Assuredly, I say to you among those born of women there has not risen one greater than John the Baptist." John must have lived a mostly selfless and obedient life for Jesus to say that about him. The hidden years of John the Baptist were undoubtedly powerful years of preparation.

The Shepherd Boy Who Became King

When I think of people who emerged from obscurity onto the main stage in biblical history, the first person in the Old Testament who comes to my mind is David. I will refer to David many times in this book because his life is such a powerful example of someone who lived completely sold out for God. David is also a great role model for us when it comes to navigating through and overcoming difficulties and pain (which, for him, was much of the time). I believe we can relate to David's life story as we navigate through our own seasons of hardship. As you know, life isn't always easy or fun, and we must suit up in our spiritual armor and war against the attacks of the enemy, just as David had to do both in the physical and in the spiritual aspects of his life.

David's journey from obscurity to notoriety didn't take place overnight. There were a few steps David took from his training in the sequestered fields where he tended sheep, to becoming a stand-out King who led the nation of Israel.

David was just a boy when the prophet Samuel arrived in town on the appointed day to anoint the next king of Israel. Samuel's arrival must have sent shivers throughout the city elders who most likely wondered why he had come. Was he there to enact justice upon someone, or to bring word of some kind? They never quite knew what this aged prophet with a direct line to God was up to.

As it turned out, Samuel was on a mission to find and anoint a successor to King Saul, whom God had rejected. Because of the dangerous nature of his mission, Samuel had not announced the reason for his visit, only that he had come to worship. Proceeding with caution, he discreetly invited Jesse, the father of David, to the festivities, knowing that from among his eight sons God had chosen a man to replace Saul as king of Israel. However, after seven of Jesse's sons passed before Samuel the chosen one wasn't there. Ironically, David – Jesse's youngest son – was never even considered a candidate by Jesse. Only when Samuel asked, "Have you any other sons?" did Jesse respond, "Oh yes, there is one other in the field keeping the sheep." When David finally appeared before Samuel, God told Samuel, "Arise, anoint him, for this is the one" (1 Samuel 16:10-12). Such is the record of David's life throughout those early years. Overlooked, yet chosen.

David's early life resembles that of the proverbial unimportant and underestimated. His exploits caused him to be promoted, but with every promotion, those over him – whether it was his father, his brothers, or King Saul (who would eventually take him to be his armor bearer) – questioned his integrity and accused him of wrong motives.

David was loved by the people and guided by the Spirit. But some of his greatest trials and heartbreaks came from being misunderstood, hated, and hunted by Saul. Yet in all of this, David remained faithful to the core.

David was a man chosen by God and appointed to greatness. He was called out by God, progressing from his isolation as a shepherd, to a mighty warrior on the battlefield. Each step along his journey prepared him for God's ultimate call on his life as king. From being summoned to play his harp to comfort King Saul, to his famous confrontation against the giant, Goliath, David's life resounds with the ultimate possibilities available to all those living lives of obscurity.

Throughout David's life, he was a worshipper, a warrior, and a leader. He took courage from the Lord to fight the battles he would face and through the years he depended on God for direction and strength. He would stand in the face of hardship with integrity and resolve. When he fell, he humbled himself before God in repentance and never turned his heart away from God.

David became known as Israel's greatest king, but he started out as an unseen, sequestered boy in the shepherd's field. Men may have thought nothing of David, but God saw his heart when he lived in obscurity. God taught him right where he was, and from there, chose him to be mighty for Him. (You can read this account of David's life beginning in 1 Samuel 16.)

My Years of Obscurity

I grew up on a 7-acre farm in Schellville, California. It's a little suburb about 7 miles outside of Sonoma. We had no post office but there was a little airport, a gas station, a diner, and a motel. There was nothing grand about Schellville but it was and still is a nice little country community.

Today, if you drive through Schellville you'll see some beautiful wineries along the main highway where people stop for tasting as they venture into Sonoma. It's quite beautiful as the vineyards sweep over the rolling hills.

Some of the original eucalyptus trees are still standing and scattered along the highway. They are tall and majestic and are beautiful landmarks to the area and the climate. To this day, the smell of eucalyptus takes me back to this place of my childhood.

The road I lived on still bears a sign saying "Not a Through Road" because it ends at the base of rolling hills. I didn't think much about it while growing up, but it was a beautiful place to live – backed up against an untouched majestic hillside with plenty of places to explore. As a kid, I felt very sequestered while living there. It was a small community of neighbors and there were a lot of open fields nearby where cows and horses grazed. It was a special place in which to grow up.

There are many things I remember about living on that country road. On our little farm there were chickens, cows, horses, dogs and lambs. My mother was always working on that farm. On top of running the household and feeding a large family, she painted fences, cared for the yard, and tended to the animals. She milked cows, made butter, and still had time to volunteer at her church. As a little kid, I'd sit on the grass and watch her as she would clip loads of laundry onto our massive clothesline. I can remember the strong winds of Schellville seemingly working against her as she wrangled the blue jeans to the line. She was always working and lived a life of selfless dedication to those she loved and to the people God would bring into her life and her home.

I remember the fun times we had riding horses, bikes, motorcycles, and driving old cars. I loved to walk in the ditches full of rainwater and sing in the wide-open fields. On occasion in the summer, we'd play a family game of outdoor hide-and-seek after dark. I was the littlest and usually the hardest to find and my dad would help me find a good hiding spot. My brothers would call out "Lori, where are you?" and I would answer "Here I am!" leading them right to me. (As a child, I apparently didn't understand the winning strategy of the game.)

Among my endearing memories of home, my favorite are the times we'd assemble in the living room and listen as my grandfather would read and expound on the Bible. He was the patriarch and spiritual anchor of our family.

That was my childhood and it was also my place of obscurity. Just a kid living in the country, doing chores and passing the time. However, unbeknownst to me, I was being prepared for a life outside of the simplicity of Schellville living.

What We Can Learn in Obscurity

You and I are often not aware of what God is teaching us in obscurity. I didn't realize it at the time, but my heart was taking in many gold nuggets during my years in the country. There was a lot of character building out there on the farm as I watched my parents navigate life and grow in their journey of raising a family and making a difference in the lives of so many others.

It was those years in a small country town that I witnessed love for people no matter where they came from or what they had done. I watched my parents take in the down-trodden and drug addicts. Opening their home to the homeless and hurting was a way of life for them.

During those years of obscurity, I learned how to be hospitable and share what I had. It was under the wing of my parents that I learned a good work ethic, and how to be spiritually diligent as I watched my parents trust in God for direction, finances, and everything else it took to raise a family of seven (with some strays in the mix). They were risk-takers and believers full of faith who lived the Gospel.

When it came time for me to launch out on my own, the very things I witnessed and learned in my years of obscurity were a source of guidance for me as I became a wife, mother, and eventually a pastor's wife as we entered into full time ministry after 15 years of marriage.

God was watching over me and forming my character even when I wasn't aware of Him. I didn't know it then, but God knew my destiny. He knew whom He had designed me to be and the assignments that He would give me. The same is true for you. I believe if you look back at your past, you might be able to recall ways God was shaping you and preparing you for your life today. You may not have had a pleasant childhood – it might have been rather difficult at times – but even in that, God was preparing you. Through much adversity, much is learned – even at a young age.

Maybe you're going through a season of life now in which you're feeling a bit obscure, due to sickness, a divorce, financial hardship, or the loss of a job. These can be difficult times of transition. You might feel unknown and unimportant and even uncared for. But let me assure you that your Unseen Bodyguard *sees* you, He *knows* you, and He *loves* you. And just like He watched over you in the past, He will watch over you today in your present. We don't always see how God is working in our situations, and we may not know what His plan is at any given time, but we can be certain that He is always working on our behalf. He certainly has a good plan for you.

Take a few moments to read Psalm 139. This Psalm has been like medicine to my spirit many times, and I will refer back to portions of this Psalm throughout this book.

Here are the first six verses:

"O Lord You have searched me and known me. You know my sitting down and my rising up; You understand my thought afar off. You comprehend my path and my lying down. And are acquainted with all my ways. For there is not a word on my tongue, but behold, O Lord You know it altogether. You have hedged me behind and before, and laid Your hand upon me. Such knowledge is too wonderful for me; It is high I cannot attain it."

David, the writer of this Psalm, was comforted by the knowledge that God was protecting him, understood him, and was guiding his life. God knew everything there was to know about David and He knows everything there is to know about you and what you're going through. I know life can be painful, but those seasons come and go. We need to remind ourselves, like David did, that we are abundantly loved by a big amazing God. We may not see Him at work, and we may not always feel Him, but He's always watching over us and moving us forward even during difficult times. Remember, He knows right where you are at this moment in your life. And He is *with* you!

Beth's Story

I have a friend, whom I'll call Beth, who wasn't given all of the advantages growing up that I had. Her years of obscurity were quite the opposite. I've asked her to tell you her story:

I was born on the East Coast into a marriage that was doomed to fail. I was the second of three children. My parents' tumultuous marriage ended with a separation when I was four. My mother took

28

my baby brother and moved to California leaving me and my older brother with my father; which was a good thing. He was a good man. And those were the best four years for me as a child. We didn't see my mother much after she left us. A custody battle ensued after she left that lasted four years. When my mother remarried, my father lost the custody battle and we were forced from the security of his home into the nightmare of my mother's home in California.

Life with my mother and stepfather was very different than life with my real father. We learned early on to stay quiet and out of the way. We also learned my mother would embellish stories so that we would receive unwarranted punishment from my stepfather. My stepfather had a large leather belt, and he liked to use it on us. We spent a lot of time alone exploring the back woods near our house in the country. It was the only place of peace for me and my brothers. My stepfather would host parties with my mother that would consist of drugs, alcohol, gambling and porn. This was such a drastic change in my life from the years with my father. I longed to be back with him every day. But I had no way of getting back to him.

Living life with my mother brought a better understanding as to why my dad fought so hard for us during those years of the custody battle. He knew the pain we would suffer being in my mother's home.

One day, I was riding the bus home from school. The ride was usually an hour long which was fine with me because it was peaceful and I could lose myself in my thoughts. I was a tired little girl, I was scared, and I felt so alone.

I remember this particular day was cloudy and rainy. It was a thunderstorm kind of day; some of the clouds were dark and gloomy and some were huge, white and puffy. I remember being hunched down into my seat, staring into the clouds, watching them move slowly as one would collide into another. In my 9-year-old mind, I wondered how things could possibly get worse and tears fell from my eyes.

I continued to watch the sky. And in that moment of my deepest *despair, I saw Him in the clouds. I saw a glimpse of His glory. I felt His presence around me and I felt His peace. I wasn't sure who He was in this moment but this was something greater and more magnificent than I could ever explain. I hadn't felt this feeling before. There was power. I felt safe. I knew somehow, I was going to be okay.*

In the years to come I would cling to that moment, knowing that there was something greater beyond where I was. And looking back, I can see how God carried me through many years of obscurity until the day came when I found Him fully. Those years of hardship gave me a spirit of tenacity and toughness. I traveled through life with much heartache as I went through a tumultuous marriage of my own, and was eventually left to raise my four children on my own. The pain in my marriage eventually led me to my church where I would finally enter into a relationship with the God who sustained me all those years. He was wooing me to come close, assuring me that He would never leave me. He assured me that the God I caught a glimpse of that day on the bus so long ago would guide me, protect me, and make something beautiful of my life.

Today I can say He has brought beauty from the ashes in my life (Isaiah 61:3). I live with a healed heart and I am whole. I have come to know Him fully and I live with a deep abiding peace.

God is Still There

I'm happy to tell you that God brought a husband – a wonderful God-loving man – into Beth's life. She recently graduated college and is now an elementary school teacher. Beth's years of obscurity were not easy years. But looking back, she can now see that those years were a training ground.

Beth said: "I learned how to press through. I learned how to never give up. I learned to hold on to hope and believe that there is always a better way. And I learned that God has commissioned me to show compassion and love as I come into contact with hurting people in my life, whether it's in the classroom or in my church or with my family. If we'll let Him, God will use what we have gone through to help others along the way."

Beth sees 2 Corinthians 1:3-4 as her life verse because of its description of how God comforted her:

"Blessed be the God and Father of our Lord Jesus Christ, the father of mercies and God of all comfort, who comforts us in all our tribulation, that we may be able to comfort those who are in any trouble, with the comfort with which we ourselves are comforted by God."

So, you see, my friend, no matter what our individual stories, no matter how obscure our beginnings, one thing we have in common is that God was there. He saw you then, He gave you strength and endurance and taught you many things. He might have even showed Himself to you in ways you weren't expecting Him to. And what about today? I can assure you He will do for you today what He's done before... He will lead you to your purpose, and He will bless you.

Embracing the God Who Notices You

1. Read Psalm 139:1-12. Write down three or four ways God notices you – even if you still feel you're in obscurity.

2. Read the following passages and record in the spaces below your response to the God who sees and knows you.

Psalm 139:13-14: "For You formed my inward parts; You covered me in my mother's womb. I will praise You for I am fearfully and wonderfully made. Marvelous are Your works, And that my soul knows very well."

My response:

Psalm 139:16-17: "Your eyes saw my substance, being yet unformed. And in Your book, they all were written, the days fashioned for me, when as yet there were none of them. How precious also are Your thoughts O God. How great is the sum of them."

My response:

3. Those verses you just read were part of David's response to the God who knew Him intimately. Now you try it. Write a few lines, praising or acknowledging the God who saw you from your days of obscurity and still sees you today.

Trust in His Unseen Work

Every one of us has had times of feeling unnoticed, hidden, or insignificant, and more than likely from time to time have found ourselves back in that place of feeling sequestered and alone. If you are in a season of seclusion, remember that if you'll seek Him, God will use these times of obscurity to accomplish great things in you. For surely it is the unseen work of the Lord in our lives, that eventually promotes us to the place of our destiny.

3

He Assures You
of Your Purpose

Have you ever had one of those weeks (or years) when it seems like everything is going wrong? (I know what you're thinking – that was most of 2020, right?) You were walking through life, minding your business, and one thing after another started to go south. It can feel like there are roadblocks, setbacks, and hurdles stacking up against you. It's times like those when it takes a lot of grit to overcome the negativity, keep the faith, and maintain the right attitude.

A few years ago, I went through a record-breaking season of setbacks. It was painful and exhausting. I was feeling overwhelmed by an increasingly demanding schedule and the many people around me who were going through their own challenges. I was carrying stress and sadness in my heart over ministry changes we were experiencing, and just when I felt that life was returning to normal, we lost our church's coffee house to a fire.

Common Ground Coffee House was a special place. It was a gathering place we had been dreaming of for years. Our desire was to have a place in our community where we could connect with people outside the walls of the church. It became everything my husband and I – and our church – dreamed of and more.

Jesus sent His disciples into the world. They didn't hang out in the synagogue every day – they went to the people, they went out into the streets, towns, highways and byways. There are many ways to go *into the world* as Jesus instructed His followers in Mark 16:15 and Common Ground was one delightful way we were doing that.

In the late '90s my husband's search for a space to broaden our reach took him to a 2,500-square-foot empty store front on the main street in our town. It was in bad shape, but we knew it was the perfect spot for what we needed. After negotiations with the landlord, our church congregation rallied and went to work. We remodeled and began bringing the space to life, and Kingsburg Youth Center was born.

When my husband, Pete, first laid his eyes on the space his dream was to create a coffee shop, but it wasn't time for that. It was time to reach the youth in our community. So, for 15 years it was a place where pre-teens and teens gathered. For eight of those years we opened every day after school for the elementary and junior high students to have a place to complete homework, play games, eat snacks, and hang out with friends. It was a sweet time getting to know the youth of our city.

When the after-school foot traffic began to lessen, we went through another remodel and kept the evening youth programs going. Our youth leadership team created what they called The Lounge for the junior high and high school groups. Our youth team spent a few fun years living the dream in their own created space. However, with the exception of staff meetings, and counseling appointments, the space sat empty most of the day. We knew that wasn't good stewardship of the property. So, feeling like we had finally assembled a good *coffee house* team, we were ready to take the leap of faith into the long-awaited goal of opening a coffee shop on Draper Street in Kingsburg.

The plan was to operate a coffee house for the community by day and facilitate our youth programs and Celebrate Recovery meetings at night. It was a plan that came together nicely. Common Ground Coffee House was filled with opportunities for outreach.

A Dream Come True

It was an exciting day when Pete announced to our church that it was time to turn the downtown space into a coffee shop. As he cast the vision on that Sunday morning, I took a deep breath. I knew it would require more money than we had, but I also knew my husband and could trust his ability to hear from God. Besides, as my brother Ben always says, "If God orders it, He'll pay for it." So, even if it was to be a slow process, we believed it was time for our dream of a coffee shop to be realized. Once again, the members of our church rallied, people in our community rallied, our family rallied, everybody was *all* in.

I remember the night I was getting ready to lead worship at our annual women's conference. I received an awesome text message from my husband. He sent a picture of a $25,000 check. I almost fell off my piano bench! A gentleman who attends our church knocked on our door, handed my husband the check and said, "Pastor, I believe I've heard from God and I've got to give this check to you. I believe in what you want to do, and this will get us started." We were blown away at how quickly God sent the start-up provision.

Pete strapped on his carpenter's belt, gathered our church troops, and moved forward in faith. We knew it would probably take four times that amount of money to do the job, but we had enough to start, and start we did.

Many people in our church worked at their day jobs, or went to school, and then came to work at the shop in the evenings or on weekends, or both. It was encouraging to see the army of God working together, sacrificing their time and finances to create a beautiful space for our community. God provided in so many ways. Many people in the community gave toward the project as well as family members and our faithful crew at church. Telling this story brings up many fond memories and much gratitude for all that God did through the body of Christ at Common Ground Coffee House.

In the coffee shop's fourth year of operation there was a lot of momentum and the place began to take off. Sales were growing. New friends from near and far were pouring through our door. It was an exciting time and a pleasure to be serving our community.

The vision for a coffee house had come into full view. It was a place where God did such wonderful things. Young people met Jesus there for the first time, formed lifelong friendships, learned to serve and work, as well as participate in lots of fun shenanigans. Travelers were introduced to Kingsburg because they found on Yelp a *nearby coffee shop* to visit while driving down the 99 freeway. People from many different countries stopped in, and even though we didn't always speak the same language we could see the look of awe on their faces upon entering the shop, then a big thumbs up at the taste of their drinks. Pastors brought their parishioners in for chats, and Bible study groups in the building were the norm. Moms came together with their littles for coffee and play dates. Musicians presented concerts and children preformed their first piano recitals. One young man held his first art exhibit in the shop to raise funds for a mission trip.

To some, it was a nice place to stop for coffee while on their travels. To others is was a place to relax and connect with family and friends. To us it was home. It was where God touched lives, especially ours.

And then it was gone.

The Loss of a Dream

On a warm night in October, I sent the crew home after our weekly Friday night guest musician had finished playing a wonderful set for our customers. I wanted to do some deep cleaning and prep work for the Saturday morning crew that would be opening at 6 am. I remember praying over the shop and enjoying some alone time with Jesus there. When I was done, I gathered the barista towels for laundering, and before locking the door, I took one last look around, and said to God, "I will never get tired of looking at this beautiful place." I whispered a prayer of thanks as I locked the door, not realizing it would be the last time.

It was just after 12 midnight when we got the call that the coffee house was on fire! My first thought was *I see another renovation in our future*. But, as I rounded a corner while heading to the shop, still three miles outside of town, I saw the sky full of a red hue from the flames and the billows of smoke. My heart sank. It was apparent there would be no fixing the coffee house, and the space would no longer be part of who we were. It was a *horrible* feeling in the pit of my stomach.

We stood on the street for hours watching our place burn, leaving only a shell. Over 15 years of memories flooded my mind as I watched the flames reaching high into the sky. The fire started somehow, (we still don't know the cause) in the second story of an adjacent business within the building, and proceeded to take out the whole building, which was a two-story hotel that was just over 100 years old. It was a landmark in our town and a tragedy to see it destroyed.

In one evening, our dream place of ministry became a memory. Of all the disappoint-ments and setbacks we had experienced, this was one of the most heartbreaking.

Remembering the Good

One morning a couple of weeks after the fire I was feeling particularly down. I felt like I was in mourning. I missed our little coffee shop. I missed the people who frequented it. I missed the ministry that had been happening there. I missed being in the community with happy, peaceful vibes, and great-tasting coffee drinks. It was a painful time of transition.

I began reminiscing about the ministry that took place in that building through the years. I thought about the people who were saved or encouraged there as teenagers during the Youth Center days, or the grieving parents who had lost their children who had been ministered to there, or the college students who loved studying there. My mind recalled the people who had been married there, and the customers who showed up regularly for their morning cup of coffee. That was the loss for which I grieved: The people. The ministry. The purpose.

On that morning, as I was sitting in my yard with tears running down my face, I felt I was sinking into a pit of sorrow. I questioned God about our purpose and how we would recover from this setback. Losing that space felt like a wing of our church had been destroyed. Much ministry had taken place there for all those years. We used it for a myriad of purposes.

I wondered why we were going through this devastation and change; it felt unreal. Then I looked up and noticed the birds in our large walnut tree. Their chirping was loud, and they were fluttering about as they were flying in and out of their homes. There were more birds lined up in a row on the power line chattering at each other. They were coming and going as they pleased.

As I watched the birds, I thought, *What a sweet, simple life. The life of a bird. How I long for that simplicity.* And then I thought, *Oh, to be a bird – to fly free and to be unencumbered by life's trials and pain. It would be wonderful to be free like a bird.*

As I sat there contemplating how easy the birds have it, I heard the Lord speak to my heart:

You're not a bird! You have an eternal purpose for My glory. Pull yourself together and keep marching forward. Forget what was behind and strive for what is ahead. My purpose for you hasn't changed.

I knew my heart had heard the voice of truth once again. The truth – and reminder – that I have an *eternal impact and purpose* sunk deep into my heart. Immediately, my perspective changed. The loss of our place wasn't a setback, it was a change in direction. It was an ending of a season. It would always be remembered as a place where we walked in faith and obedience. Many lives had been touched there and for that we could rejoice.

I leaned back in my chair, and I took a deep breath of fresh perspective and hope. I admired my backyard neighbors as they were taking their flight, and I decided I was going to take my own flight – the flight into my future of divine purpose, with renewed strength and with a grateful heart. It was time to move forward and remember why I am here on this earth.

Our Job is to Trust

Sometimes we won't be able to reconcile why God allows things to happen in our lives. The roads we travel have the potential to be full of twists and turns, hills and valleys, and some things we'll never understand. It's not our job (or even our right) to know the reason for everything that happens. Our job is to simply trust the One who paved the road before us, trust the One who holds the answers, and trust the One who has called us and placed within us an eternal purpose.

The day I was sitting in my yard, God had to remind me my identity and my purpose wasn't in a building or a business, or a ministry. My identity and purpose is in Christ, who lives in me. I carry within me the purpose and calling of God wherever I go.

My purpose and yours is very simple—to follow Jesus, and to bring Him to a world that is hurting and lost. Our purpose isn't hinged on the things in this world. Sure, we're in the world, we occupy spaces, we have careers, launch businesses, get married, and have families. But, as you know, sometimes life throws a curve ball, and our tidy world can be interrupted. We face tragedies, we face death, marriages fail, businesses fall apart, friendships end, and fires burn… None of these circumstances affect our purpose.

God will never change His mind about why you are here on this earth. You are to be a light for Him. Jesus said, "You are the light of the world. A city set on a hill cannot be hidden; nor does anyone light a lamp and put it under a basket, but on the lampstand, and it gives light to all who are in the house. Let your light shine before men in such a way that they may see your good works, and glorify your Father who is in heaven" (Matthew 5:14-16 NASB). Wherever God brings you, or whatever He puts in your heart to do, be a light. Nothing that happens in your life changes that purpose. God's love for you is immeasurable, and He desires that you walk in your God-given calling.

I think of King David again, and how he was a man who lived his purpose, yet he had his times of sin, setback, and unfair treatment from his enemies. I can relate to his song in Psalm 55. It sounds like he was in a difficult place and feeling like he had sunk to the bottom of his pit when he penned these lines of his song:

"My heart is in anguish within me;
the terrors of death have fallen on me.
Fear and trembling have beset me;
horror has overwhelmed me.
I said, "Oh, that I had the wings of a dove!
I would fly away and be at rest. I would flee far
away and stay in the desert;
I would hurry to my place of shelter,
far from the tempest and storm" (verses 4-8 NIV).

Apparently, I'm not the only one who wished I was a bird. David did, too! I appreciate how David didn't try to hide what he was going through or how miserable he felt. He had the ability to be transparent with emotional pain and times of weakness. We aren't alone in having to navigate through battles, and it's not unusual to want to escape from hardship (and literally fly away from it like a bird), but what we find in David's life (and our own) is God doesn't call us to escape. God calls us to trust Him, to remember our purpose, and then lean on Him.

Another attribute I admire about David, is that in his writings he turned full circle in prayer. He declared the goodness of God, the ability of God, and the hope of God. He proclaimed his praise and love for God, even in desperate times. After crying out in despair and wishing for escape, he ends his song with a simple declaration: "But I will trust in You." What a powerful example he was. He stands and declares what he knows for sure – he belongs to God, and he can trust in Him in the worst of times.

A Wheel Within a Wheel

I think of the purpose and calling of God as being like a wheel within a wheel. God's purpose is universal, the overall plan (the outer wheel), and God's calling is how God uses each of us with our individual talents, interests, gifts and so on (the inner wheel). If you're not sure about your calling, remember He uses who you are, and what you love, with the gifts He's placed within you. You've been designed by Him to be an important part of His purpose and to impact others for eternity.

God's got a lot of lanes on His highway. And there are a lot of off-ramps going from that highway into *all the world*. When you step back and look at how God uses the body of Christ, with this perspective it's quite amazing to see the *wheel of God* working.

God Hasn't Changed His Mind

If you're experiencing what you believe are setbacks or maybe you've recently come out of a time of hurt and disappointment, I pray you'll be encouraged by the reminder that God hasn't changed His mind about you or about your purpose and calling. His plans for you are still good (Jeremiah 29:11). Trust Him, the One who paved the road and the One who put the gifts within you to navigate with Him, through the journey.

As difficult as setbacks and transitions can be, you are not defeated. The enemy of your soul would love for you to believe God doesn't care about you or what you're going through. Yet nothing could be further from the truth. It's important to remember that God is for you. He's called you to have an eternal impact on the world around you. Taking flight is not an option. You're not a bird.

Focusing on Your Purpose

1. Read Ephesians chapter 1. How many times in this chapter are the words *in Him* recorded?

From this passage, what benefits do we have by being *in Him*? List them in the space below.

How do verses 17-19 help you in regard to your calling?

2. According to verses 19-23, where is Jesus now? And who does He have authority over?

How does this affect you as a believer?

3. Second Thessalonians 1:11-12 is about your calling and purpose as a follower of Christ. List the various aspects of your purpose that you find in this verse.

Changing Your Perspective

The day God gave me the revelation about purpose and calling as I was sitting in my yard watching the birds, I chose to look at our coffee house experience differently. I needed to change my perspective and quit dwelling on the pain and disappointment of the past. I needed to thank God for the positive things the past held, as well. What did the past hold? The past held obedience to God and a successful leap of faith. The past held the will of God. The past held God's provision and strength and a lot of lessons. The past held trusting in people, and the past held many years of meaningful ministry in a storefront space where God allowed us to realize a wonderful dream. We did our very best with what He gave us. These are all important and precious aspects of the past, where the purpose and the calling were fulfilled as we rolled down the highway of God.

If you struggle with overcoming disappointment from your past, ask God to give you a new perspective by revealing to you all the *good* things He accomplished for you in that place of setback.

He has equipped you, through Jesus, to move forward with certainty and an overcoming spirit. What you do for Him has the potential to make an eternal difference for those around you, and that's worth every setback, hurdle, or roadblock that you may encounter. Always remember, your purpose and calling stand firm in Christ.

4

He Helps You
Step Over Intimidation

I sing. It's what I've done all my life.

I'm not famous. I don't give concerts or sing in stadiums, or in front of thousands of people. I don't possess that kind of talent, nor am I called to that type of platform. The closest I've been to fame was being asked to sing for a local radio show. I must admit, it was fun to hear my performance on the local station as my husband and I were driving to church one Sunday morning.

Then there was the time I was asked to sing in someone's restaurant during the dinner hour, in the lounge. The lounge was where the bar was, but it was also where people ate dinner. It was an awkward experience for me, and I was glad when it was over. Hearing intoxicated men in one booth loudly proclaiming during a song, "Well, praise the Lord" and other dinner guests clanking utensils and trying to have conversations while I was singing in the corner about Jesus, just wasn't my cup of tea.

From my earliest years, I can remember loving music and singing whenever I was alone. My horse was my audience; the open fields and country roads were my stage. I can still remember how much I loved the feeling of the wind blowing through my hair as I sang my favorite Karen Carpenter songs.

When I was a little girl, we attended the First Baptist Church in downtown Sonoma. Just about every Sunday I would watch in awe and curiosity as the choir director would stand and wave his arms back and forth in grandiose movements. He would point at certain singers keeping them on track to sing their parts. They sounded beautiful as their voices blended in harmony. Watching and listening to the choir was my favorite part of going to church.

One Sunday, I was so inspired by the choir director that, upon returning home, I went into my bedroom and pretended to lead my own choir. With my back to the doorway, my arms were flying through the air, pointing to individual objects in the room, as if to call on them to sing their parts with precision. After bringing the "song" to an end, I gave a dramatic bow, arms falling to the ground with an *it is finished* exhale. And then came the applause. *Literally.*

My parents had been standing in the doorway watching my performance! They were clapping and smiling as if I'd just completed a concert at Carnegie Hall. I was only about six, but I remember feeling embarrassed and yet pleased at the same time. I ran to them and stood in the middle of them and put an arm around each one. As I did, they wrapped their arms around me and made the circle complete. I was the youngest of five children in the Hardister clan. My parents were busy raising a family, working and running life on the farm, but for just that brief moment I had them both to myself in grand approval, even if my achievement was imaginary.

I don't think my parents knew, as they stood in the doorway that day, how much music would become a part of my life. God had planted a love for music in my heart at a young age and I went from leading a choir made up of dolls and stuffed animals, to being in a choir during elementary school. While preforming in concerts, I paid close attention as the director would wave her arms in grandiose gestures and lead the different sections to sing their parts. On one occasion, when our school concert was over, she smiled at us and mouthed the words "I love you" and then turned to the audience and took the big bow. The crowd clapped and cheered, and again, I soaked up the feeling of approval and achievement.

Learning to Stand Alone

I was never afraid to sing in the choir as a child. I was surrounded by my peers and there was no standing alone. But when I reached my twenties that changed. Many years had passed since I'd been involved in singing and although I loved to sing, I didn't have a platform and I had no desire to sing solo. That was, until we were married and landed in a little church where the pastor's wife, Sister Sharon, began to seek me out to sing. She wouldn't be denied. She had a knack for discovering abilities in people and including them in ministry, and I was on her radar!

This was the church where I surrendered to the call to sing. It was a safe and loving environment in which to grow – except for the presence of one older gentleman. I'll call him Downer Douglas. Mr. D.D. took it upon himself to seek me out after the services and point out my flaws. I used to tell Pete, "I think he's got it out for me." It was hard enough to put myself out there without his "helpful" advice. Had I taken him seriously, I probably would not have kept showing up on the stage. Gratefully, I had a pastor and his wife who believed in me, and who pushed me forward in my love for music with words of encouragement and many opportunities to use my musical gift.

Looking back on my journey, I'm amazed at how God orchestrated my life – from a little girl who loved music, to now being a pastor's wife leading worship for more than 25 years. One step at a time, God brought me to where He wanted me to be. He knew the plans He had for me and gently led me to my calling and assignment, even with all my flaws.

Psalm 139:13-14 tells us that we are wonderfully made and that the works of His hands are marvelous. We are the *marvelous works of His hands*, and I believe our ever-present God is standing in heaven's doorway watching and cheering for us as we "direct the choir" and grow in our abilities.

Facing Down Intimidation

I think it's natural for us to become discouraged, distracted, or even fearful from pursuing our dream when we're faced with opposition or obstacles, negative people, financial woes, physical interruptions, or family issues. That's when we must remind ourselves that we are called by God and He is the One who has placed that dream or calling in our hearts. Sometimes we listen to the intimidation of the enemy and lose sight of the truth. Satan whispers thoughts like: *You're not good enough. You don't belong here. Your life is too busy to try that. No one will listen to you. That's just a dumb dream. It's too difficult for you.*

While writing this book, I battled many doubts. They took the form of thoughts like: *No one knows you. You don't have a big enough readership to be writing a book. Why would anyone read your book? You're a nobody; you're just wasting your time.*

I had to fight through those negative thoughts and doubts on several occasions during the early months of writing. Then one day, when I was sharing with a friend how I was feeling, she told me "You're listening to the voice of self-doubt and he was hired by the enemy." We laughed and I went on with my day thinking about what she had said. I knew it was true, and I had to ask myself, *Would God be saying those things to me?* The answer was no. Remember, He's a Father who stands proudly in the doorway, smiling with love and approval as His child endeavors to try something new.

Overcoming Your Obstacles and Fears

Early on, my obstacle was the old gentleman, Mr. Downer, at my church who pointed out my flaws every time I sang. I had to learn to give his voice no room in my head. I'm sure we all have stories about well-meaning people who were actually sowing seeds of doubt and fear in our hearts and fueling the insecurities within us. Sadly, some of us let insecurity and fear win, and we stop pursuing our dreams.

As I have struggled – and as I've watched others struggle with achieving new milestones and goals – I've come to believe that the obstacles we face are often gifts. Obstacles can force us to dig deep, examine ourselves, and discover who we are. If we look at obstacles from the right vantage point, they can put a fire in our spirit and give us the nudge to keep striving and working toward our goals.

I'll never forget the time I was asked to sing a solo at a large church conference. My first emotion was intimidation because the solos were usually sung by people who had been attending the conferences for a long time. You know, the people who are super talented, or who are in the inner circle of leadership. I was neither. So, I felt out of my league. But I couldn't turn down what I felt God wanted me to do. So, I committed to going.

On the evening I was to sing my solo, I was brought backstage before the service began, to wait my turn to sing. I walked behind the curtain to find my seat among the other women who were also waiting; they were the visiting ministers' wives and some of the officials' wives (you know, the "bigwigs"). They looked very official and sophisticated. They were sitting in a row and they all looked my way when I entered *their* space.

They were all much older than I was. They wore fancy clothes and lots of jewels. They wore their hair in poufy updos like a beehive-type style. I was the complete opposite of them; I was in my early 30s and wore my hair down in a 1970s feathered Farrah Fawcett style. I wasn't wearing fancy clothes or sparkly jewels, but I was fine with that. I remember thinking, *we're all on the same team* because they were there to do something for the service, too. I walked up to them with a big smile and said "hello!" The women didn't respond. Not a hello, not even a smile. It was quite the contrary. I got a stare-down-the-nose look as if they were all thinking, *What are you doing here?*

I stood there for a moment feeling awkward and small. I was unwelcomed in that space. I believe they wanted to let me know that *only the important people are supposed to be backstage.* I wanted to leave, but I knew I couldn't. I had already committed to sing. As I sat down, I was still in shock at these Christian women who were so rude to the new kid. As I sat there in silence, wanting to disappear, the enemy taunted me with that ugly voice of self-doubt and intimidation: *What are you doing here? You don't belong here. You're not one of these people; you're getting ready to make a fool of yourself.*

It doesn't take intimidation long to show up, does it? The enemy doesn't want us to move forward and realize our dreams or do anything noteworthy for God. Whether it's getting more involved at church, starting a new business, pursuing a new career, going back to school, or standing on a platform you've never stood on before, when you decide to step out, don't be surprised if intimidation whispers accusations in your ear. In my story, he made sure there were people there to compound my feelings of insecurity.

Have you ever been there? Have you ever started a new plan in life with excitement and hope just to get broadsided with intimidation and ended up feeling like crawling under a rock? That was me as I sat in that chair trying to muster up the courage to do what I was asked to do – to simply sing a song. I began to pray, *Lord why did You open this door for me? I feel like a fool. Why did You put me here?* And then I heard Him speak to my heart: *You're right, I put you here. They did not. One day you will be in a place of leadership…remember what this treatment feels like. Now get up and sing for Me.*

A Man Named Gideon

Gideon was an Israelite living in a time when the nation of Israel had walked away from God. The Bible says the Israelites did "evil in the sight of the Lord, so the Lord delivered them into the hand of Midian for seven years" (Judges 6:1). The Israelites had a track record of leaving God through disobedience and then returning to God in repentance when times were tough. He was a merciful Father and would forgive their sin and bring them into a right relationship with Him once again. This seemed to be a cycle for the Nation of Israel. The story of Gideon takes place during one of those cycles of rebellion.

For seven years, the Midianites would oppress the Israelites by stealing their produce and livestock and leaving them impoverished. The Midianites were a mean bunch and were very large in number, and like the locusts of that day, they would leave the land in devastation. Imagine replenishing your food and livestock, just to have this brutal army come through and take it all again, year after year. The day finally came when the Israelites had their fill of the Midianites and once again, they began to cry out to God. And once again, God heard their cry.

This is where we meet Gideon. Some believe Gideon was a coward, because Scripture tells us he would hide in a winepress and thresh wheat, in order to keep it from the Midianites, and to provide for his family. I think he was a man of ingenuity and courage because of those very reasons. Was he afraid? Probably. But that doesn't make him a coward. He might have felt like a coward. He might have been depressed or discouraged. He might have felt like there was little hope for him and his nation. But cowardice? I don't think so.

One day, while threshing wheat in his hiding place, God sent an angel with a message for Gideon. The angel said, "The Lord is with you, you mighty man of valor." Gideon was baffled and replied with some questions. To paraphrase, he said something like:

"If God is with us, why has all of this happened to us?

"And where are all the miracles our fathers told us about?

"It seems like God has forsaken us and given us into our enemy's hands. Is that true?"

The angel simply said, "Go in this might of yours. And you shall save Israel from the hand of the Midianites. Have I not sent you?"

Gideon's reply reminds me of my own self-talk at times. He said, "O my Lord, how can I save Israel? Indeed, my clan is the weakest in Manasseh, and I am the least in my father's house." The angel assured him that he would defeat the enemy. (This story is found in Judges 6:11-16.)

Even with this promise from God, Gideon still doubted and asked for a sign to confirm that he'd found favor with God to do this mighty thing. After all, it seemed an impossible feat.

If you read the entire account of Gideon beginning in Judges 6, you'll find that Gideon received the reassurance he needed and the plan of God to move forward into battle. He led a small army of only 300 men against thousands of mighty Midianites. It's a fascinating, miraculous story. God showed up bigtime for Gideon and the nation of Israel and brought them victory, just as He promised.

It would be easy to be intimidated if you or I were in Gideon's circumstances. God was calling him to get out of the safety of his hiding place and go into the battle. Not just any battle, but in Gideon's eyes it was a battle in which he was badly outnumbered. Then, there was the fact that his clan was the weakest in the nation, and he was the least in his family. No wonder he asked God for a sign. I'd want confirmation, too, if I were Gideon. Yet, God took him step by step from intimidation to a place of preparedness and courage. The intimidation factor in Gideon's life was real and frightening. God called Gideon – the one who was the least, but who was also doing something in the midst of the mess. Gideon was doing what he could – hiding and threshing wheat – when God stepped up and helped him do what he couldn't. God called Gideon to step over the top of intimidation and into courage.

Bringing it Home

Looking back at the day I was sitting backstage among the poufy-haired ladies, I realize He called me to do the same. When I heard God whisper His truth in my heart, I relaxed and took a deep breath.

I breathed in confidence and I exhaled out the feelings of doubt and intimidation. I was so grateful to the Lord for speaking to me in that moment. Every feeling of inadequacy left me. I knew I'd heard from God. I knew He called me to be courageous. When it came my time to sing, I walked across the stage to the podium, took the microphone, and sang my heart out. In doing so, I tossed aside the disapproval of strangers and intimidation. And there, in that moment on a stage before 800 of my peers, it was just Jesus and me. It was an awesome feeling of stepping over the top of intimidation into courage.

How are *you* handling intimidation right now? I'm sure if we were sitting across the table from one another you could tell me some of your life stories about being intimidated. Maybe you're in a season of life right now in which you are facing many obstacles. What I've discovered is that intimidation can stop us only if we let it. That's the plan of the enemy – to stop you dead in your tracks and steal your freedom. He'd love to take from you your ideas, or new relationships, or new careers, or a new ministry. *Don't let him.* God has equipped you to rise above your enemy and see past the temporary obstacles that come your way. Whether the challenges before you are big or small, it makes no difference because God sees you, just as He saw Gideon. He is with you, and He knows the potential He's placed within you to succeed.

For the moment, you and I can be quite intimidated by a situation or a person who appears to hold power over us. That's when we need to remember the truth of who we are and Whose we are. For me, those women were momentarily an obstacle. I had to process and dig deep to overcome intimidation and realize they had no power over me at all. God used that experience in my life to teach me these lessons:

- When intimidation comes, stop and pray. Don't look around, *look up.*
- When God invites you in, it doesn't matter what people think. People don't call you, *God* does.

- Other people's ideas of position and importance don't determine your worth or calling.
- In the presence of your obstacle, give God all you've got. Jump over fear and *do it*. Then shake the dust off and don't look back.
- Not everyone welcomes you. That's okay.
- Be nice to the new kid. We're equally important in God's eyes.

Stepping into Courage

1. In what areas of your life are *you* facing intimidation?

Can you define *why* you're feeling intimidated? If so, write it in the space below.

After reading the story of Gideon's life in Judges chapter 6, what do you sense the Holy Spirit speaking into your heart about your own intimation factor?

2. What do you need to do to step over intimidation?

3. Read Psalm 121 and record in the space below the promises of God that build your confidence and courage.

Listen for the Truth

Into every life, sooner or later, intimidation comes. It may be a fleeting feeling at the precipice of a new challenge or a crippling fear that grips your heart and renders you ineffective. But, as you cry out to God, and spend time in His presence through His Word, He will speak truth to your heart. The more you look up toward the power of God, instead of looking aside at the intimidation of the enemy, the more your confidence will grow. And, one by one, your battles will be won, and you will become less and less intimidated.

The more you step over intimidation, the more the enemy loses his grip in that area of your life. Keep up the good fight, my friend, one hurdle at a time, and pretty soon you'll look over your shoulder and see how wonderfully far you've come. I hope you leave this chapter knowing that fear is a liar and God hasn't called you to be spiritually crippled by fear. He also hasn't called you to hold conversations with self-doubt. Remember, the voice of self-doubt was hired by the enemy! Start a new habit of listening to the loving voice of Truth.

5

He Promises You
He'll Never Leave

I 've found much comfort in the fact that Jesus promised you and I, we would never be alone.

There's a passage in Matthew that I've always loved. Jesus was talking to His disciples right before He went to Heaven and He simply said, "Lo, I am with you always, even to the end of the age" (Matthew 28:20). What a great promise for Jesus to make as He was commissioning His followers to take the Gospel to unbelievers throughout the world. He knew the road ahead of them wasn't going to be an easy one. They would face difficulties and even persecution (many of them to the point of death) as they carried the message of salvation through Christ to the world. Jesus wanted them to know through all their hardships, He would always be with them. And He wants you and me to know the same thing today. He is with us, *even to the end of the age*.

The fact that Jesus is with me is not a promise I have to remind myself of every day. I don't pace the floor feeling anxious, wondering if Jesus is with me. I know He is. His Spirit lives in me. Most days I sail through life doing my job, loving my family, and hopefully meeting challenges and helping others to do the same. (Here's where the *but* comes into play…)

But, there have been times in my life – when the uncertainties stack up, or the heat of life gets turned up through adversity – that I've asked God, "Where are You in this?" Trying to navigate through the storms can feel overwhelming. Sometimes when my prayers aren't answered right away and it seems like the storm is prevailing against me, I'm tempted to wonder if God is paying attention to what's going on in my life.

Have *you* been there? I've listened to a lot of people in my career as a pastor's wife who've asked me these same questions: "Where is God?" and "Doesn't He realize how much I'm hurting?"

I think it's common to have those moments of anguish when we're suffering through something.

As I mentioned in chapter two, King David is one of my favorite people in the Bible. Even though he was a mighty warrior and a man after God's own heart, he had his moments of lamenting before God. He expressed himself in many songs (psalms) as he processed his emotional pain. If ever there was a guy who went through some difficult years, it was David. He cried out to God and said things like "How long, Lord, will You hide Yourself forever?" (Psalm 89:46). David wasn't shy about questioning God in his moments of anguish. But he was also vocal about how God was his Deliverer and his Strong Provider, rescuing him from his enemies.

Sometimes, it can feel like God is nowhere to be found. But that isn't the truth. He is always with us no matter what we may feel and no matter what our circumstance may be. He is *there.*

God is omnipresent, meaning His presence is everywhere – He cannot be confined or contained. He lives inside of every believer, through the indwelling Holy Spirit. God is also with us through His vast army of followers – other believers like you and me. He shows up in our lives by using people to convey His wisdom, His warmth, His presence, and His support. There have been times in my life when a person has shown up right when I've needed someone, or God will send someone with a word of revelation that speaks to my heart in a way that only God could. He uses us to pray for one another, give to each other, lead, and love each other. He loves us through the comfort of His people.

My Need for Peace

Two years into our marriage, Pete and I discovered we were going to have our first baby. This development wasn't planned, but we were excited, and early in the pregnancy we were planning for our baby's arrival. We were very aware that we were already a family of three. I purchased baby books to read about where my little treasure was in his or her development, began thinking of names, and started to read books on good parenting skills. It was a very sweet time for us.

One morning, a couple of months into my pregnancy I began to have physical problems. I called the doctor and was instructed to take it easy, stay off my feet, and keep her informed. With each passing day my issues worsened. After a few days of no improvement I went to the doctor's office where I ended up miscarrying on the examining table.

The feeling of losing our child in that moment was unexplainable. We were heartbroken. It was one of those times when I wondered where God was. Even though I knew in my head He was there, I felt like He was so far away at that moment. Later, I would look back on that morning and realize it was His presence in my life that was carrying me *through* that pain.

During my exam that day, the doctor felt a swelling in my fallopian tube that appeared to be an infection, so she put me on antibiotics and sent me home. A week after recuperating, I got up one morning to get ready to go back to work. As I showered a tremendous pain enveloped my stomach. I had never experienced pain like that before. I barely made it back to bed without fainting. We had no idea what was happening, but we assumed it had something to do with the miscarriage. Once again, we called the doctor and once again she instructed us to come right in to be examined, as she suspected the new development wasn't good. I couldn't elevate my head without fainting and the pain was severe. I was doing everything I knew to simply breathe and relax as I laid flat on my back in the back seat of the car for the 20-minute ride. Upon our arrival, the doctor examined me, and then explained that the lump she felt in my fallopian tube at the first visit wasn't an infection, it was a baby and my tube had burst! I was bleeding internally. Her final thought on the matter was that I had two babies. One in the uterus and one in the fallopian tube. It was a lot to take in as I was fighting to stay conscious and also manage the pain. This would be something I would process after I was out of danger and safely through the ordeal of this first horrible pregnancy experience.

My husband swept me up off the examining table and once again carried me to the car where we would rush to the hospital for my emergency surgery. It was a stressful situation and with every passing minute fear was trying to take hold of my mind. I was whisked into the operating room and while waiting for surgery to begin, I was having difficulty breathing. I'd been bleeding internally for more than an hour and I felt like I was dying. It took everything in me to breathe deeply and not let fear overtake me. I was struggling and felt very scared, alone, and very much like I was losing a battle. And *then* it happened. God sent His presence and reassurance in the form of an anesthesiologist.

My anesthesiologist entered the room and when he did, I could feel his confidence and peace. He had a very calm demeanor. He leaned over the operating table so he could make eye contact with me, introduced himself, and told me what his job was. Then he looked into my eyes and said, "Lori, let's pray." I whispered in my shaking, scared voice "please do." I don't remember the words he prayed, but I do remember that *when* he started praying, a calm and a peace came over me. He said very quietly, "now just breathe deeply, you're going to be okay." And I believed him. God sent just the right anesthesiologist to the hospital for me that day. My Heavenly Father and Bodyguard knew I was going to need someone to bring me peace and reassurance as I laid there on that gurney wondering if I was going to die. It didn't matter to me that I didn't know that man. What mattered was that God was there, calming my fears, through the prayers of a caring stranger.

God's Powerful Presence

That would not be the last time God would visit me during the disappointment and grief of that failed pregnancy. For three years after that experience fear would revisit me and I fought a private battle trying to overcome it. Not only were my chances of getting pregnant cut in half, but I fought the fear that if I did conceive, the same horrible thing would happen again. Even though God had seen me through the ordeal of near death, and even though He sent a stranger my way for comfort, the fear for me was, if it happened once, it could happen again. The *what ifs* kept creeping into my mind. The enemy of my soul was doing his best to steal my peace, and I did my best to ignore him, but it was a struggle…until the night I had a life-changing encounter with the Holy Spirit.

I was at a Bible study at my sister's house. At the end of every study, we finished the evening in a prayer circle. As I was standing in the circle quietly praying, I thought about my fear issue. I thought about asking for prayer, but didn't feel ready to share my struggle with everyone there, so once again I shoved it down and put it away. I stood there silently, listening to others pray when out of nowhere my body became overwhelmed by the presence of God. The room felt like it was slightly spinning and I lost all strength. I fell to my knees and then flat on my back.

As I laid there on the floor, my whole body began to tingle. I knew what I was experiencing was a *holy visitation*. I felt the presence of God like I never had before. I couldn't move, I felt paralyzed. The tingling in my body began to intensify all over. The sensation went from my head, to my hands, through my body, to my feet. It was the strangest feeling and I started laughing at the thought of what was happening to me and crying in awe, at the same time. I laid there like that for a few minutes. I was taking in the supernatural presence of God. After a few minutes, the tingling in my body began to travel. It moved from being everywhere to gathering just in my stomach. As the tingling sensation hovered over me, I knew the Lord was healing me physically, emotionally, and spiritually. I knew He was removing all fear from my heart about future childbearing. I wept there on the floor in my husband's arms as the tingling subsided and the peace of God was securely planted in my heart.

That was approximately 36 years ago, and I remember it like it was yesterday. I got up from the floor that night, a different person. I experienced no more pregnancy fears, through the power of His presence.

A couple of years after that experience, I gave birth to our first son, Brandon, and three years after Brandon, came our second son, Joshua. God, in His grace, gave us two strong boys who have grown to be two amazing men.

God's Angelic Army

The Bible is full of stories in which God sent His angels to minister to, instruct, protect, guide, and fight for His people. (See Genesis 3:24; Exodus 14:10; Numbers 22:24; 1 Kings 19:5-7; 1 Chronicles 14:13-18; Matthew 4:11; and Luke 22:43, for several examples.) God's vast army of angels is described in Psalm 103:21 as *His hosts*, or *Ministers of His who do His pleasure*. In Psalm 104:4, the angelic hosts are referred to as *spirits, His ministers a flaming fire*. From the beginning of our time on earth, angels have been a part of God's plan. From the events in Genesis to today, the Heavenly Hosts, the Ministers, have been very busy.

I'm encouraged by an Old Testament story in the book of Second Kings in which God was there in the midst of a battle, when His servants most needed Him to show up.

Elisha was facing a tough situation one day in Dothan. The King of Syria had sent an army to apprehend Elisha, the prophet of God. The Syrian army had surrounded Dothan during the night, standing ready to capture Elisha. So, there they were in all their might with horses and chariots, like bigshots, surrounding Elisha and his servant.

To be surrounded by such an army would be terrifying, and it was for Elisha's servant, who was concerned that they were badly outnumbered by this great army. However, the Prophet Elisha knew God was with them and His Angel Army far outnumbered the enemy's army. So, Elisha prayed to his God. First, he prayed for his servant's eyes to be opened so his fears would be calmed. Secondly, Elijah prayed for the enemy to be blinded. God did both.

Let's look at this portion of the story in 2 Kings 6:15-17:

"And when the servant of the man of God arose early and went out, there was an army, surrounding the city with horses and chariots. And his servant said to him, "alas, my master! What shall we do?" So, he answered, "Do not fear, for those who are with us are more than those who are with them." And [Elisha] prayed, and said, "Lord, I pray, open his eyes that he may see." Then the Lord opened the eyes of the young man, and he saw, and behold, the mountain was full of horses and chariots of *fire* all around Elisha."

I've often wondered how it must have felt to be the servant, and how it must have impacted him for his eyes to be opened to see supernaturally the might of God in the form of His angels surrounding them. I'm sure the sight of the Angel Army of God must have brought a great peace and much courage to him and Elisha. And He probably never looked at adversity the same after that. The words of Elisha, "Do not fear, for those who are with us are more than those who are with them," were words he probably recalled every time he was faced a fearful situation.

It's good for us to remember that God hasn't changed. Not only is He always with us, but He still sends His ministers as a flame of fire on our behalf. That means what He did for Elisha, He can do for you. When your back is against the wall, and the battle seems to be overwhelming, remember that God has an Angel Army and He sends His warriors forth like ministers or a flame of fire to fight for you. You are never alone, no matter how difficult life may seem or how impossible a situation may feel. God is with you through His Angelic Hosts. He sends them on assignment just as He did in the stories we read about in the Bible. Psalm 91:11 tells us "For He shall give His angels charge over you, to keep you in all your ways."

I've never literally seen an angel of God, but I know that every promise in the Book is mine and therefore, God has led or protected me through His unseen army. Without a doubt I believe this.

I regularly pray for God to dispatch His Mighty Angel Army to do His good pleasure in my life and to also protect my family and our ministry. Prayer is the key. We pray to God and God commands His army to go to work. I believe the great *visible* army of God, His Body, is also a powerful force on this earth. God uses people like you and me to show the world His presence and to get things done. If you look back on your life, I'm sure there are stories you could tell about the supernatural moving of God through people in your life or those who've crossed your path. You know exactly what I'm talking about, don't you? Or, maybe God has used you as the vessel to meet the needs of someone else.

Then there are also those times in the wee hours of the morning when it's just you and the Holy Spirit as you sit and pray in your living room chair, or lie awake and pray in bed, and you know beyond a doubt He is there and He will answer. Quietly, powerfully, He comes. Jesus is with you always.

Recognizing God in Your Midst

1. Can you remember a time when you were convinced God sent a person to meet your need (like He did for me in that operating room)?

How does it make you feel to know that God, the Creator of Heaven and Earth, cared enough to send help your way?

2. In the chart below, list how you were feeling before you received that person's help and how you were feeling after. (I've completed the first line for you.)

Before help arrived:
I felt fearful, anxious, sad

After receiving help:
I felt relieved, grateful

3. In the space below, write a prayer of gratitude to the Lord for the special way He met with you through another person.

4. What advice would you give someone who claims he or she cannot feel God during difficult times?

5. Summarize the following Scriptures and note what they all have in common:

Genesis 24:40:

Genesis 19:15:

Numbers 22:35:

Acts 5:19-20:

You Are Never Alone

Whatever you may be facing today – whether it's a financial, a physical, an emotional, or a relational need – His presence knows no bounds and He will help. Whether it's through a person, or His Angel Army, or the power of the Holy Spirit, He will meet you in your time of need.

For me, I was fighting a quiet battle of fear only He and I knew about. There were times I succumbed to the enemy's lies and felt very alone. Waves of sadness and grief mixed with fear and doubt would dominate my thoughts. I had prayed about this battle many times and waited on the Lord. It was through the power of His Holy Spirit on the floor of my sister's house that He wiped away my fear. That is how He chose to remind me I wasn't alone. It was a miraculous display of His glory, and it was something that changed my life.

For Elisha's servant, God's reminder of His presence came through the unveiling of the natural sight and getting a peek at the supernatural army of Heaven. It must have been amazing to see such a vast army, ready for battle. Talk about not being alone!

God doesn't always choose to work in a dramatic, supernatural way as he did for Elisha's servant and as He did for me. Most of the time, God will show you that you are not alone through a simple song on the radio, or a conversation with a friend, or a sermon your pastor may preach, or through insights and understanding as you're reading His Word. He has a multitude of ways to remind you He is with you. And He often uses ways that He knows will best reach you right where you are.

Remember friend, you are precious to Him and you are never alone. Jesus' promise to you is that He will never leave you, nor forsake you (Hebrews 13:5) and He will always be with you, even until the end of time. May the words of Elisha resound in your spirit today:

"Do not fear, for those who are with us are more than those who are with them."

You are surrounded by His mighty presence.

6

He Provides for You – Always

Have you ever hesitated to ask God for help with what seemed to be an impossible need?

Sometimes, without realizing it, we put parameters around what we believe God can do and what we believe is in the realm of the impossible. We can tend to ask Him for things we think He can deliver, but hold off on the things that are too "out there" or impossible. There have been times in my life when doubt has been subtle and has crept into my thinking and I've had to shake myself back to reality and remind myself that anything is possible with God.

God's Word asks, "Is anything too difficult for the Lord?" (Genesis 18:14). The answer is *no*! A wholehearted, resounding *no*!

I love to hear stories of when God shows up in supernatural ways, using His people to meet needs. God has a vast army of followers who are tuned into His spiritual frequency. When you think about it, how else is God going to provide? He doesn't tend to use the *"coins in the fish"* method anymore (Matthew 17:24-27). Today, He uses people to accomplish His miracles.

When my husband said he had heard from God in prayer about landscaping our church property, it was an exciting day. But, it was also a bit unnerving. I was excited about the possibility of finally beautifying our property and seeing my husband's landscaping vision come alive. This was a desire we'd had for a long time, to improve the curb appeal of the church. We'd been waiting to tackle the grounds due to the cost factor. It was a blank slate of ground with just grass, nothing appealing about the "triangle" as we call it (because it's a triangular piece of property). The unnerving part about this project was the fact that we didn't have all the money up front for the expenses involved. Pete felt it was time to move in faith with what we had, and he was confident that since God was leading us to beautify the property, He'd make a way for us to pull together the rest of the finances we needed.

So, the church landscaping crew started tearing up grass, and we began to shop for large rocks, plants, and trees. We envisioned having several big rocks for people to sit on and lots of trees to provide shade. It was to be like a park, full of charm and ambiance.

Just as we started tearing up the lawn and getting ready to purchase some costly "sitting rocks," we discovered the church was infested with termites. Tackling this problem was not in the beautification plan, nor was it in our skimpy budget. But, it was something we couldn't ignore, so we gave the go-ahead to the pest control company to tent the building and treat the pests, not knowing how we'd be able to pay for that on top of the landscaping work we were already committed to completing. Yet, we had peace about moving forward in faith. We prayed and kept working.

The day before the termite tent went up, I was at the church and my phone rang. It was my brother, Ben.

"What's going on?" he asked.

"Nothing much, just working at the church," I replied. "Why?"

"Well," he said, "I need your mailing address. I was praying this morning and the Lord told me to send you $10,000 to help with ministry costs."

I was *blown away*. I told my brother everything that was going on, and he replied with a simple matter-of-fact statement: "Apparently, God doesn't want you to worry about how you're going to get this project done."

It was one of those phone calls in which you hang up and then ask yourself, *did that just happen*? I'm certain that God gets great pleasure out of the *wow factor* that goes on in our hearts after He comes through in big ways.

God made a way for us through someone who had the ability to hear from Him concerning finances. The extra funds from my brother, when added to our own finances, paid for *everything* we needed to complete the job – termites and all.

What a great lesson it was to us about operating in faith. It was also a memorable example of how God uses His army to get His work done. From small projects like ours to big projects needing millions of dollars, faith in God is the key. God is pleased by our faith – faith to believe Him for what we need, and faith to give of what we have to meet someone else's need. I don't think my brother had a lot of extra money lying around. Giving $10,000 was a sacrifice for him, but he made it happen, because the Lord had a need for it. Our God knew there was a little church, on a little triangle of land, in a little town, stepping out in big faith to beautify His house.

God's vision and provision for our landscaping turned out to be a perfect plan and we are now enjoying the park-like feel of the church grounds. Every time I approach our church property, I take in the ambiance of the beautiful landscaping and I smile. I remember what happened to make it possible and I whisper a prayer of thanks to God for His provision.

Incidentally, a few years after the completion of our landscaping project, we received a letter from the city manager thanking us, as a church, for our part in beautifying the city of Kingsburg with the landscaping of our property. That was God – using people to bless people. His army, His provision, His perfect work was evident.

Serving in God's Army

Each one of us has a talent, ability, and finances we can be using for the Lord. Every soldier, every position, every skill is needed and important.

If our church family wasn't full of willing, hard-working individuals, that story (and the landscaping) wouldn't have looked quite the same. It took men to tear out our existing lawn, build mounds for planting, lay concrete, place rocks, plant the trees, and rearrange the sprinkler system. That project took finances and muscle power. I think that's what I love so much about our little park – we didn't have to hire any labor for the job. The labor came from a small section of the body of Christ coming together to make it happen. There is power in the ranks. I've seen our church people rally together on so many occasions it's been mind-blowing. It has been a great privilege to armor up and carry the torch with our people at New Life Ministries.

First Corinthians 12 lists the gifts of the body of Christ, and the importance of each member of the body. In God's scheme of things, there is no one who is insignificant. Everyone is equally needed and treasured. As a matter of fact, as I've discussed earlier in this book, many times God uses the small and humble, *the least of these*, to get His work done. He also uses the mighty and strong. We are *all* a part of His plan.

The Giving Factor

Scripture teaches that every one of us is called to give of our finances to build God's kingdom. Some are called to give more than others, but everyone is called to give. I've known millionaires who write big checks with no hesitancy to further the work of God. What a blessing these people are. But I also know single mothers who are barely making ends meet who will not think twice about whether they should tithe on their paychecks or give to a missionary. Their obedience to give of their finances is a stretch for them, financially, and it hurts. But they give regardless. I aspire to have faith like theirs.

Many years ago, when we were going through one of those *stretching* seasons with our finances, we were asked to speak at a friend's church. It was time to receive the offering and as I was writing the check, I felt the nudge from God to raise our intended offering from $25 which wasn't much of a stretch, and give a little more. *Take it to $50* was my thought. Now $50 may not seem like a lot, but that day it was for us. I wrote the $50-check, and put it in the offering plate, knowing that God honors faith, even at the $50-level!

After ministering to the people there at the church, my husband and I prepared to leave. As we were saying our goodbyes, the church secretary walked up and handed my husband a check. We tried to hand it back, but she wasn't allowing that, so we gratefully received the offering. When I looked at the check on the drive home it was for $500! God blessed us with *ten times more* than what we gave in that offering. This I know for sure, we can't out give God!

I realize, in the scope of things, this is a small example of how God gives back. But it was a memorable example to us of God's provision and a big lesson to us of a principle of giving: When your finances are stretched, stretch yourself to give.

You may think you don't have enough to give to God. But think of the widow in the Bible who gave all she had. Jesus gave her an honorable mention and used her for a teaching moment in Mark 12:41-44. The rich had put money into the temple treasury out of their abundance, but the poor widow gave all she had.

"So He called His disciples to Himself and said to them, "Assuredly, I say to you that this poor widow has put in more than all those who have given to the treasury; for they all put in out of their abundance, but she out of her poverty put in all that she had, her whole livelihood" (verses 43-44).

Once again, we read in the Scriptures, that what seems to be the least, is the greatest in God's eyes. Don't ever think your small gift doesn't matter, or that it's not enough to make a difference. No matter the size, your obedience is what counts and it counts for a lot. God will bless your obedience and use you and your gift of giving to do His work.

Giving finances is part of being in the army of God, and as you give, this is your promise from the Scriptures:

"Give and it will be given to you: good measure, pressed down, shaken together, and running over will be put into your bosom. For with the same measure that you use, it will be measured back to you" (Luke 6:38).

Micah 3:10 also attaches a promise to giving:

"Bring all the tithe into the storehouse, that there may be food in My house, and try me now in this," says the Lord of hosts, "if I will not open for you the windows of Heaven and pour out for you such a blessing that there will not be room enough to receive it."

Nowhere in Scripture will you find that God only expects the wealthy to give. This command to give willingly and generously is for all. The blessings attached to these verses aren't contingent on the wealth of the giver, but rather the *obedience* of the giver.

Therefore, if you have a need, and you don't know how you're going to make it, try sowing a financial offering. Maybe you haven't been a giver because you don't think you can afford to give. If that's the case, let me assure you that God will bless you when you decide to walk in obedience to His Word and give. It is a command, and as you line up with His commands concerning your finances you will have your own stories to tell about how God multiplied *your* offering.

Trust God with your money. Go ahead and tithe on your income. Cast your bread upon the waters (Ecclesiastes 11:1) and see what God will do for you as He returns it to you *pressed down, shaken together and running over*. That's a *full* cup of blessings!

A Bin of Flour and a Jar of Oil

God seems to enjoy taking what little we have and doing big things with it. Take for example the widow of Zarephath in 1 Kings 17. She was a widow who gave all she had, but she didn't give of her finances. She gave all she had left in her pantry – a bin of flour and a jar of oil.

She lived during the reign of Ahab, king of Israel. Ahab was an ungodly king and he was a poor leader who lived a compromised life. Ahab's wife, Jezebel, was a wicked woman and played a large part in why he was such an ungodly king. As a result of Ahab and Jezebel's sin, the nation of Israel had fallen into deep spiritual depravity. That is when Elijah entered the scene.

Elijah was God's prophet and God used him to call His people back to Himself. God told Elijah to go to Ahab and pronounce His judgment and call for a famine to consume the whole land of Israel. After doing so, Elijah retreated to a brook in the wilderness where God provided for him. But after a while, because of the drought, the brook dried up, leaving Elijah looking for somewhere else to go. The famine was severe and there were no Walmarts or produce markets to provide food and water like we have today. People were very dependent on the seasons in those days and no rain meant everyone suffered, even Elijah.

Elijah asked God what his next move should be, and God told him to go to Zarephath where there was a widowed woman whom He'd commanded to take care of Elijah. When Elijah arrived, he found the widow just outside the city, gathering sticks to make a fire. She only had enough flour and oil to make one last meal for her and her son to eat before they died of hunger. Elijah told her to first bring him a morsel of bread. Her reply was, "As the Lord lives, I do not have bread, only a handful of flour in a bin, and a little oil in a jar; and see, I am gathering a couple of sticks that I may go in and prepare it for myself and my son, that we may eat and die" (1 Kings 17:12).

That poor woman was down to nothing. Imagine her predicament. All she had left was enough for one last bite. Perhaps you've never been in such a desperate state. Perhaps you've never known the empty feeling of having a barren cupboard. Or perhaps you know that empty feeling; you've felt the sting of not having enough. Thank God He is our unseen Bodyguard in both times of plenty and times of want.

That is a truth that the widow discovered. After the woman informed Elijah of her desperate situation, Elijah didn't apologize, nor placate her fears, nor did he respond with concern for her plight. Not at all.

Elijah's reply to the widow was both a challenge and a promise: "Do not fear; go and do as you have said, but make me a small cake from it first, and bring it to me; and afterward make some for yourself and your son. For thus says the Lord God of Israel: 'The bin of flour shall not be used up, nor shall the jar of oil run dry, until the day the Lord sends rain on the earth'" (1 Kings 17:13-14).

In an act of blind faith and complete obedience, the widow did exactly as Elijah commanded and the Lord was true to His word. The flour in the bin and the oil in the jar remained. Each time she opened the bin and jar, she miraculously found more. I believe that when God's anointed man, Elijah, prophesied to her, a spark of hope must have been lit in her spirit. She took his words "Do not fear" and moved forward in faith. God, in turn, took her faith and gave her abundance in place of her lack.

God had His sights set on this widowed woman. He knew her state of desperation and He knew that even in her hardship she would dare to trust and believe. God knows *your* heart, too. He knows the fears you may be facing. He knows if you've got enough to make it to the end of the month. He knows if you're alone and struggling. Just as He spoke to the woman in this story, He speaks the same words to you today: "Do not fear." He is with you and He will provide for you. He's your Father and He hears the cries of your heart.

God blesses the activity of giving. I encourage you to try it. Try exercising some *giving faith*. I'm not suggesting that you empty your bank account and give it all to the ministry, but maybe start with simply designating a portion of every paycheck to God's work. That is a good starting place. Then, let God speak to your heart about the other areas in your life where you can give – such as giving of your time by serving voluntarily at your church, or helping a friend in need. Maybe,

God would like you to bring a meal to a family who is struggling. There are so many ways to give…and as you do, you will see what He will do with your bin of flour and your jar of oil.

Giving of Yourself

1. Think of an area in your life in which you are having trouble trusting God. Maybe you are having difficulty believing Him for something. What is it? (As you write it down in the space below, that is one way of releasing it to Him.)

Why do you think you struggle with trusting God with this particular situation or area of your life?

2. Read the following verses and next to each reference write down why God can be trusted or what you learn about God's faithfulness, ability, and guidance as you trust in Him. Are there instructions in these verses for you? If so, what are they?

Matthew 7:7-11:

Matthew 21:22:

Psalm 9:10:

Psalm 18:30-31:

Psalm 37:5:

Proverbs 3:1-10:

3. List your talents, interests, and passions below and indicate how you are using them to serve others. (As you do, think about how you can improve your service.)

My talents, interests, passions:

How I can use them to serve others:

4. How is the giving factor in your life? Pray about it for a few minutes and write below what God seems to be saying to your heart.

Trusting Your Provider

Where God guides, He provides. Sometimes, it can be a challenge to remember that promise, but it's true. He's a God who always comes through.

Be careful that you don't push God's instructions aside, thinking *What if I proceed and God doesn't come through?* He is One who takes care of His children, His church, and the needs we have. He inspires the creative thought and the plan, and He provides the finances, the willpower, and the muscle power to get it done, through His people.

God also comes, not as a mighty army, but sometimes as a still small voice in the middle of the night, because He knows when you just need His reassurance. In those quiet moments, He whispers His promises: *You're going to be okay. I will see you through. I hear your prayer.* He provides for your heart by bringing hope, courage, and strength when you are weary. He's mindful of every area of your life, and He is the One who gives you the faith to believe. He will meet you right where you are, and He will bless you as you endeavor to exercise your faith and put your trust in Him.

My prayer for you today is that you will be reassured of God's presence in every aspect of your life. Whether you need moral support, financial support, or something material, may He quickly send in the troops – or His quiet assurance – to help.

7

He Walks You
through the Weeds

We like to think of our Bodyguard, our Good Shepherd, as one who leads us through green pastures and along quiet streams. It's a nice picture. And, while He does just that, green pastures and quiet streams aren't the only paths He guides us along or accompanies us through.

According to Psalm 23, our Good Shepherd also walks us through the valley of the shadow of death, which can be some pretty rough terrain. There have been times in my walk when I've felt like I'm trekking through a valley of the shadow of death-type of terrain, and I have wondered if the green pastures and still waters would ever return. Thank God, they do.

I was on a walk through our peach orchard with our dogs recently when the dogs and I traversed some rough terrain. It was a beautiful morning. The air had a pre-Autumn fragrance and was crisp and delightful. I love signs of the seasons changing. At this time of year on the ranch, harvesting is finished, and the orchards are at rest. The ground is furrowed and watered, the weeds stand proud and tall like sentries barring the path ahead. There are rotting peach culls scattered throughout the ground, and on occasion there are broken branches in the path. Late summertime in the orchard can feel a little bit like a jungle.

As I was walking, I had my two pups, Molly (a Pitbull mix) and Mickey (a shepherd) on either side of me. Buster is my Akita-St.

Bernard mix, and he usually trails behind as he is the "senior citizen," and likes to take his time. Usually, we have to stop a few times during our walk to let him catch up. I will often say to the pups, "Where's Buster?" and they will stop and turn to look for him. (It's quite cute.) But on this particular day, Buster decided he was going to lead the pack. I was surprised as he came from behind in a nice trot to move past us. Up to the front of the line, he went.

He was jogging at a good pace when we came upon a patch of weeds. They were dense and wet with dew. This patch of weeds wasn't pleasant, but Buster plowed through them, not fazed at all by their texture, wetness, height, or the fact that he temporarily couldn't see up ahead to the other side. He knew where He was going. He must have known the weeds were temporal. And so, he kept his pace.

Then, Buster came upon a couple of rotting peaches. His big paws brushed against them, and he never lost his stride as they rolled aside. The peaches were simply a minor nuisance.

Along with the weeds and the peaches, came an occasional broken branch. Buster kept moving forward, hopping over every twig. He kept his stride, no matter what was in his path. I thought to myself, *Boy, Buster dog has had a lot of obstacles on his journey this morning, and he just keeps going.* He was unhindered and unfazed by what surrounded him. We eventually came to the end of the obstacle-ridden path, onto a country avenue where the road was smooth and clear.

Our Own Trek through Weeds

I think our lives can sometimes look like Buster's trek through the peach orchard. We've got our plans as we travel through life. Even though we may not always clearly see what lies in front of us, we're pretty sure we know how to get through the path ahead. Our terrain isn't always easy, clear, or pleasant. There are hills and valleys, and most assuredly we face obstacles, and sometimes one after another. At times, we struggle with navigating the obstacles, thinking if we try harder, or force our way through out of sheer determination, we'll be fine. Other times, we cringe at the thought of entering difficult terrain and new territory so we shrink back and stand still. Or worse yet, we turn around and go backwards.

I've experienced my own times of traveling through rough terrain. I try my best to know God's will and fulfill what I think His plans are for me, but there are times along the way when I feel like I'm in the weeds. Can you relate to what I'm talking about? Weed patches are a common occurrence as we try to keep our lives in balance while walking the path which, at times, can feel like an unwelcomed obstacle course. Sometimes, our vision is impaired by the tall weeds of distractions, worries, and life's pressures that loom before us. It can be so difficult to see through them from where we are to where we're going.

Are you, like me, at times, trying to perfect the balancing act? It's simply part of our lives, isn't it? You may have a career both away from the home and in the home. If so, I salute you. That amounts to doing double duty and you should be congratulated for having a two-career status. The challenges of everyday life are exhausting for most of us. We are trying to keep a marriage healthy, raise God-fearing children, keep the boss happy, keep ahead of the laundry, keep the fridge stocked, and put decent meals on the table. And, let's not forget church attendance and the support and service we give in that area. You might be caring for your aging parents, while dealing with age yourself, and all the *wonderful* dynamics of menopause (sigh). And if you're a single mom? Single parenthood adds a whole other dimension to this list. (And, I'd be remiss not to mention keeping up with kids' sports, homework, and school activities.) Talk about living in a jungle! Can you see why, from time to time, you may run into a patch of weeds? You are busy and dealing with many different aspects of life.

I think a journey through the weeds can be brought on by several conditions. It can be the feeling like you've hit an emotional wall. You know, the feeling of being overwhelmed with the demands of life and how they outweigh your energy level? I know when I'm feeling exhausted the demands of life appear to be magnified.

Some of my times of trekking through the weeds have been when I've been unable to shake off discouragement, self-doubt, disappointment, or frustration brought on by a prolonged trial or a period of loss or pain. Those seasons of our lives can bring feelings of depression and uncertainty. It's uncomfortable, and we can lose our ability to see the way out.

Like Buster, you start out doing your best to step over the obstacles that lie in the path (like ugly fears or any one of the emotions I mentioned). At the same time, you attempt to hop over new challenges that make moving forward difficult. That's the balancing act we do so well as women. That is where trusting Jesus comes in to play. Spending time with Him regularly helps me remember the beauty of my journey, and that the weeds are temporal. There is a way out, and I'm not alone – my Bodyguard is with me, and He gives me the power to overcome and keep my pace. The same is true for you. No matter what fear or hesitation you feel, or what obstacles surround you, He is walking with you – watching your feet so you don't stumble. Can you almost hear Him softly speaking? *Keep moving forward, don't lose your stride; you're almost through this patch.*

Sometimes you and I find ourselves in the weeds because we've grown weary. There can be an underlying feeling that something's got to give and it's usually the thing that's not screaming at you. It's easy to let up on your time with God when the stress level is on overload. But, let me assure you that Jesus is the One you need. Skipping your time with Him is not the answer. The power of His presence helps you see through to the other side of the weeds where the path becomes manageable once again.

In God's Grip

In Psalm 17, David said in the midst of opposition that was all around him: "My steps have held to your paths; my feet have not stumbled" (verse 5, NASB).

And in Psalm 37:23-24, he sang:

"The Lord makes firm the steps of the one who delights in him; *though he may stumble, he will not fall*, for the Lord upholds him with his hand" (NASB).

In the New International Version, that verse reads:

"The steps of a man are established by the Lord,

And He delights in his way.

When he falls, he will not be hurled headlong,

Because the Lord is the One who holds his hand."

I *love* that! The Lord – my Bodyguard – is the One who *holds my hand* – and yours. Look at that phrase in another translation:

"If he stumbles, he's not down for long;

God has a grip on his hand" (Psalm 37:24, MSG).

I rely on that grip, don't you? Through the weeds, the sticks, and the rotting fruit – whatever that may represent in my life and yours – He's got His grip on us.

Where Are You Walking?

Are you on an uncertain path right now? Are you finding the weeds rise so tall you can't see where you're going or what's on the other side? Perhaps you know where you're going but there are sticks and rotting fruit along the way that you're having a difficult time stepping over it all. Trust the Lord, my friend, that if He has called you on this path, He will protect you on it, as well. And if you're on a path that you don't necessarily think God placed you on, but you got there on your own, take heart – He knows how to get you on the right path. He hears the longing of your heart and your earnest prayer.

Following His Lead

In Psalm 16:11, David recorded for us the promise that accompanies us as we walk His path:

"You will show me the path of life; In Your presence is fullness of joy; At Your right hand are pleasures forevermore."

1. What "tough terrain" have you encountered recently? (Tough terrain can be as simple as being discouraged, or more intense like going through difficulties in your marriage or experiencing the death of a loved one.)

2. Where did you (or do you) see God working within it, guiding you through it, or whispering words of encouragement?

3. Sometimes God speaks through His Word or leaves us with an impression on our hearts, or even uses a pastor's sermon or a conversation with a friend, to encourage or guide us. Think on this and write down the last time God spoke to you during your time of struggling through your tough patch of weeds.

4. Write out the following verses in your preferred translation of the Bible and circle one (or more) that are the most helpful to you. Psalm 119:11:

Romans 8:35-39:

1 Corinthians 15:57:

Hebrews 12:1:

1 John 5:4-5:

Now type the most helpful verse(s) into your phone, put it on your device's screen saver, or write it on a notecard and post it where you will see it often. Better yet, memorize it as a way of hiding God's Word in your heart.

Clearing the Path

As you walk with God, you don't have to, nor will you always, see past the weed patch you may find yourself in. You also won't be able to avoid the pain of obstacles, at times. The key is to trust that your Bodyguard is with you on your journey, and He knows how to get you to where He's called you. As you trust Him, you'll surely learn to push past the fear of the unknown, and the trials that come your way on that uncertain path. As you deepen your trust in Him, you'll get better and better at hopping over the obstacles that lie before you, and, like Buster the dog, push them aside and trot right past them. Through the experience you gain as you walk with God, you'll be able to keep your stride no matter what the terrain is like.

Always remember that just like I could see over the top of Buster to the path ahead, your Bodyguard can also see the path ahead of you.

He sees every obstacle you're headed for, and the tough terrain that awaits, but He also knows how He's going to bring you through.

Pray this prayer with me as you trek through tough terrain:

Lord,

I'm so grateful that You are near me in every part of my journey. I am confident that You lead me beside the still waters and restore my soul, but You also walk me through those dark and uncertain places, too. I choose to trust that You will make all things work together for my good, because I love You and am called according to Your purpose (Romans 8:28). I know You are with me and You see where I'm going, and You know how to get me there. I trust You today with every part of my life. As the Psalmist prayed, "Uphold my steps in Your paths, that my footsteps may not slip" (Psalm 17:5), "And lead me in the way everlasting" (Psalm 139:24).

8

He Comforts You in Your Pain

My husband and I have experienced more joy than I can describe during our more than two decades of leading a church and ministering to people.

I've often described our experience in ministry by saying, "We've been fortunate to have a front-row seat in the grandstands, watching as God changes lives."

From performing wedding ceremonies, to helping restore marriages, to celebrating the birth of babies, and best of all witnessing people being set free as they come to know Jesus as their personal Savior and Lord, it's an exciting adventure to help people navigate through life and watch them grow.

But there have also been times when I've felt like that traveler in Jesus' parable who was on his way from Jerusalem to Jericho when he was ambushed by thieves. He was stripped, beaten, and left for dead on the side of the road. Fortunately for him, a passing Samaritan stopped to bandage his wounds and ministered to his needs (Luke 10:25-37).

Being "ambushed" today can be brutal. These kinds of attacks take you by surprise and knock the wind out of your sails, because unlike the parable Jesus told, these attacks usually don't come from strangers who seek to take our money. They come from people within our ranks – our churches and ministries, our families, or our circles of friends.

King David was well aware of this kind of grief and ambush when he wrote many Psalms about personal betrayal. In Psalm 55:12-14 he wrote:

"For it is not an enemy who reproaches me; Then I could bear it. Nor is it one who hates me who has exalted himself against me; Then I could hide from him. But it was you, a man my equal, my companion and my acquaintance. We took sweet counsel together and walked to the house of God in the throng."

It aches to the core to be hurt by people you thought were on your team. The knife penetrates deeper when it comes from the hand of someone you thought you could trust. A person on the outside of your circle can't really impact you that deeply. Oh, but those whom you call family, or work closely with, or worship alongside, or break bread with, or call friends? Those are the ones who can truly break your heart.

Have you ever found yourself in that place of deep wounding? Are you there now? If so, my friend, this chapter is for you. Perhaps you are still struggling to forgive. Maybe you are still searching for healing from that pain. My prayer is that I may be for you who the "Good Samaritan" was for the dying man on the way to Jericho.

I wish I could sit next to you and speak words of life and encouragement into your spirit. Since I cannot physically be there, allow me to share my heart and speak truth to you through my written words instead.

Betrayal is one of the most difficult wounds to heal from. And it's a difficult one to forgive because betrayal can have many angles to it and cut deeply at many levels. If you're in the middle of a hurtful situation and are wondering *Why am I not over this yet*? don't think it's because you're a weak person, or that you're not "holy" enough. Your heart was wounded, and wounds take time to heal.

Scars Don't Form Overnight

I never thought I'd desire a scar so badly as when we went through a particular time of emotional pain. I remember wondering if there was ever going to be a scar. A scar would indicate healing, yet my wounds seemed to remain open and gaping. My desire was to skip to the scar and forget about the pain. I wondered *Would the wound always bleed, keeping the pain fresh*? I have learned that healing is a tender process and as we lean on Jesus, He guides us step by step through the valley of sadness to a place of restoration. And yes, the scar does eventually form.

I remember sitting at the patio table in my backyard trying to recover from a broken heart over an event that had happened in our ministry. My heart was so wounded and I was pondering how life had taken such a turn. It felt very diabolical. The attack of Satan, the enemy, was strong. I laid my head on the table and began to cry out to God. My spirit felt so heavy that it was hard to breathe. It was the kind of prayer in which words couldn't describe what my heart was feeling; it was deeper than forming words, it was heartbreak and I was grieving. Paul talks about this kind of prayer in Romans 8:26 when he says: "Likewise the Spirit also helps in our weaknesses. For we do not know what we should pray for as we ought, but the Spirit Himself makes intercession for us with groanings which cannot be uttered."

My husband came outside with some breakfast and found me in this state of deep sorrow. He sat in the chair next to me and began to softly pray for me. He wasn't used to seeing me this way, and I could tell he was concerned as he put his hand on my arm and sat with me. I couldn't respond to him. I couldn't lift my head. All I could do was gasp for air and weep. After a while of my husband's presence and prayers, my spirit calmed and he picked up my plate and quietly left me in the hands of the Lord.

That day Jesus wasn't telling me to stop the crying and get over it; I didn't feel His displeasure at the condition of my heart. He saw me in my pain. He wasn't telling me to pull myself up by my boot straps and march on. He was simply holding my heart and loving me. After some quiet time of meditating on His Word, I began to feel His assurance. He brought to my mind what I *knew* for certain, even though what we were going through felt so devastating. I *knew* beyond a doubt that He's the God who sees everything and knows every detail, and in the midst of our turmoil, I didn't have to explain anything to Him. He, my ever-present, all powerful Bodyguard was holding me up even though I felt like a crumbling mess. I could feel His presence almost as if He was standing there beside me, and I was comforted.

As my spirit quieted within me, I began to remind myself who my husband and I were – overcomers. And I reminded myself to Whom we belonged – God Almighty. As I pondered this reality, my cries of despair turned to cries of gratitude and hope. That day marked the beginning of my healing. Truth settled into my heart, as I declared aloud, "We're going to be okay because God knows, God understands, and God will lead us through this valley. He loves us, He is for us, and He is a faithful Father." I didn't know how He would make things better or right, I just knew He was in control of the storm, and I was able to surrender to Him my will and my heart once again.

My friend, there is power in verbally professing our condition in Christ. You may need to declare life-giving truth aloud over and over until the victory comes. So be it. Keep speaking truth. Speak faith-filled declarations of hope and surrender. Strongholds are broken as we declare the truth from God's Word. The enemy of our soul loves to taunt us with how hurt and angry we are. But God's Word reminds us that we are overcomers through the power of the Cross of Christ: "For whatever is born of God overcomes the world. And this is the victory that has overcome the world – our faith" (1 John 5:4).

Pluck Up the Seeds of Anger

Jesus was well acquainted with betrayal and rejection. Those wounds and emotions were part of what He experienced to complete God's redemptive plan. God didn't shield His Son from pain and He doesn't always shield us from it, either. It's difficult to imagine when we're in the middle of our trials that God is accomplishing good things. But on the other side of the storm, we can often see how God was working on our behalf during those painful times.

The Bible tells us Satan, our adversary, prowls about like a roaring lion seeking whom he can devour (1 Peter 5:8). Sometimes he seeks to devours us through the actions of the one who betrayed us. The enemy of our soul can use people in close proximity to us as his pawns to create division and turmoil. These pawns may not realize it, but it's the enemy who is often whispering ideas in their ears, causing them to think wrong thoughts and prodding them to act on them. Satan delights in causing division among believers in Christ and leaving them in emotional and relational pain. He wants to destroy or halt the work of the Lord. His goal is to render us ineffective. What better way to do that than to bring us to a place of bitterness as he pits one friend, spouse, co-worker, or relative against another? In fact, the enemy isn't just tempting the *offender*, he is also tempting the *wounded*. Satan works on multiple levels to bring his diabolical plan to fruition.

When you and I are wounded, we can be tempted to remain in a state of anger and un-forgiveness, and from there, allow bitterness to take root in our hearts. Seeking justice can then follow, as we tend to forget that God is the only One who can make things right when we've been wounded. In my experience, hurt turned to anger, bitterness followed, and I wanted justice. My husband explained it this way: "Anger is a seed. When that seed isn't plucked up, it takes root and that root goes deep and turns into bitterness. The root of bitterness causes nothing but trouble." And I knew he was right.

In Hebrews 12:15, we are exhorted to be "looking carefully lest anyone fall short of the grace of God; lest any root of bitterness springing up cause trouble, and by this many become defiled." Fortunately, I was able to recognize what the enemy was trying to do in my life and I knew what I needed to do with that downward spiral. I needed to repent, pull up any seed or root that had taken hold, and let the Word of God speak to my heart.

When your heart is bleeding don't seek justice… seek God! Set some time aside every day and let God's words wash over your spirit, mind, and soul. Scripture will instruct you to:

- love your enemies and pray for those who spitefully use you (Matthew 5:44).
- quickly forgive those who have offended you (Mark 11:25).
- not keep score of one's offenses or count the number of times you've forgiven them (Matthew 18:21-22).
- not take vengeance because vengeance belongs to God (Hebrews 10:30).

These are some of the great challenges of the Gospel. It's like a college class of the heart titled "Following Christ 101." Not a lot of people take this course. Sadly, many who claim to be followers of Christ attend church on Sundays and put on the happy face, but secretly harbor un-forgiveness in their hearts. They've got a long tally against people who've wronged them but expect God to forgive them of their own sin. It doesn't work that way as we read in Matthew 6:14-15. I don't believe followers of Jesus can walk in freedom while holding on to resentment (Romans 6:12). I surely couldn't. Jesus was clear when He laid out the plan to complete freedom. It's very simple and it's part of the prayer Jesus taught His disciples: Forgive as you have been forgiven (Luke 11:2-4).

Jesus also said in Matthew 15:8-9: "These people draw near to Me with their mouth, and honor Me with their lips, but their heart is far from Me. And in vain they worship Me, teaching as doctrines the commandments of men." May you and I always strive to take the words of Jesus seriously and live them; not practice mere lip service, but actually keep our hearts close to the Father in true obedience as we walk through painful trials.

Self-Examination

When I look back at difficult times in my life I am often convinced I could have done some things differently. Pain causes me to react, at times, when I should simply wait on God. But waiting on God is a tall order and I'm convinced we learn these tough lessons through trial and error. Fortunately, God is a gracious teacher and adds His forgiveness as we adjust our hearts and our behavior.

Examining ourselves is an important practice no matter what is happening in our lives. David knew this well when he prayed in Psalm 139:23-24: "Search me, O God, and know my heart; Try me, and know my anxieties: And see if there is any wicked way in me, and lead me in the way everlasting."

Examine yourself and reload your heart with the truth you find in His Word. When you are trying to overcome painful assaults, you're in a spiritual battle. *Fight smart.* Fight through the power of His Word. Look up every Bible verse you can find on forgiveness and living in Christlikeness. Read the words of Jesus and the prayers in the Psalms about overcoming emotional pain.

Don't Get Stuck in the Desert

I learned, while going through betrayal, that no one is powerful enough to thwart the plan of God for our lives. I want you, dear friend, to remember that when you *are* going through trials, as well. No demon, no person, no painful event can stop God's destiny and purpose for you. However, sometimes our own stubborn will keeps us from God's best for us. We can choose to stay tethered to anger, and become stuck, or let God take us through the process of letting go.

In Exodus 3:7-10 we read about God's plan to bring the Israelites out of Egyptian bondage and into the Promised Land. However, their own disobedience kept them wandering in the desert until a whole generation had passed away. God kept His promise – their descendants went in and took the land. But the generation He delivered from slavery in Egypt did not (Numbers 14:20-32). How sad. I want everything God has for me. I know you do, too. I pray you and I never flounder in the wilderness of disobedience, causing us to miss out on the Promised Land of our own lives because we are weighted down with the sin of unforgiveness. It really is our choice. Nothing is worth missing out on the freedom God intends for us.

As we near the close of this chapter I feel it's important to remind you of a beautiful fact. God loves us *all*! We all fall short and miss the mark (Romans 3:23). We all have our growing pains, and lessons we're learning. Your brother or sister in Christ, a relative, or friend, a husband or wife – whomever it was who hurt you – Jesus loves them, just as He loves you. Just as He desires to accomplish His work in you, He desires to accomplish it in their hearts, as well.

It's easy to fall into the trap of thinking we are the ones on the right side of God. Maybe you *are*. But that doesn't matter. God doesn't think like we do. His thoughts are higher than ours (Isaiah 55:8-11) and He sees all sides. He is unbiased in His judgment and sees where we've all been right or wrong. Our job, then, is to pray for those who are causing our suffering, to love them and not to seek vengeance. Walk through the process of letting go of the offense and leave it in God's capable hands. Your offender is not your problem. Whether your grievance is with another believer or not, God knows how to reach them. (See Matthew 5:44 and Romans 12.)

Jesus came to heal you, to make you better, and to make you a beautiful example of what it looks like to be His follower. We look the most like Jesus when we are forgiving our neighbors. So, the more mature you are in your faith, the more suffering or betrayal you've probably been through. God doesn't place us in a protective bubble. We go through life and enjoy the sunshine but also endure the storms. God didn't promise that we'd never face hardships, but He did promise to walk through them with us. He sees you in your pain and He understands. He holds your heart and stands ready to help you through to the other side where you can experience healing and forgiveness. He did it for me, and I know He will do it for you.

Trusting in the God Who Sees Your Pain

In Genesis chapters 37-46, you'll find a fascinating and inspiring story about Joseph, the second to the youngest of Jacob's sons who became one of the greatest leaders in all of Egypt. But Joseph went through some lows before he experienced the highs. Take some time to read the account of Joseph's life.

1. In the space below, list some of the ways Joseph was betrayed or let down.

2. Look again at Genesis 39:1-6 (when Joseph was in Potiphar's house) and Genesis 39:20-23 (when Joseph was in prison). What are the common elements in these two events of his life?

What would you be thinking, during those situations, if you were Joseph?

Why do you think God's favor was upon Joseph?

In all the years of Joseph's enslavement – whether it was in Potiphar's house or in the prison – Joseph walked with integrity and did what was right. He served well, and no matter where he was or how unfair his life seemed, he kept his hope in God and forgave those who wronged him. At the end of his story, we find him finally being elevated to second in command over Egypt. After all the years of turmoil, Joseph went from the prison to the palace! What a day that must have been for Joseph.

God's plan was to bring Israel's clan into Egypt. All the years of pain melted away for Joseph when he was able to see that God had a purpose and a plan – and his suffering was part of that plan. We don't find Joseph becoming bitter or angry at God or his brothers. He had a clear understanding of how God worked through him and his suffering when he said to his brothers at the end of his life in Genesis 50:20, "But as for you, you meant evil against me; but God meant it for my good, in order to bring it about as it is this day, to save many people alive."

3. Can you recall times in your life when you had to experience pain in order for God's plan to be accomplished?

If so, did you find it difficult to trust Him?

Why or why not?

4. Search your concordance at the back of your Bible (or conduct a search at BibleGateway.com) for scriptures on healing, forgiveness, and God's power and peace. Record some of them in a journal and reflect on them, prayerfully.

Healing Your Heart

If you are a follower of Christ, you are in the "Jesus Club." It's a club where Jesus is the President. He was betrayed, abandoned, rejected and so much more. Jesus wasn't waiting for an apology from Judas who betrayed him or Peter who denied him or the people who yelled "crucify him." That wasn't important to Him. What was important was the completion of His assignment – to obey His Father even unto death and by doing so, carry all sin, sickness, and disease upon His body. He became the living sacrifice for our sins and won the battle against Satan when He rose from the dead three days later to bring eternal life and freedom to everyone who would believe. What a Savior! He paid our debt of sin, and not just for you and me, but for everyone who believes – and that includes the one who has wronged you.

I know as you seek God, the Holy Spirit will help you heal. And sometimes He uses people to help walk us through that healing process. I encourage you to talk with a Bible-teaching pastor, counselor, or trusted friend who can help you forgive or get to the next level in your healing journey.

This is my prayer for you today:

Father God,

Thank You for the woman who has spent her time reading and pondering these truths from your Word. I know that You see her right where she is in her journey of faith. I'm grateful that she and I can come to You, just as we are, without fear of condemnation or rejection. You look into our hearts with love and desire and You came to heal us and to set us free; we give You praise for that!

Thank You for being the God who lifts up the broken-hearted and "gives power to the weak" and increases the strength of "those who have no might" (Isaiah 40:29). You are a great God who does mighty wonders for us, and I know You will do great things as we pursue peace and healing. Help us to recognize the seeds of anger that, if left in the soil of our hearts, will turn to bitter roots. May we quickly pluck up those seeds and learn to forgive just as You have freely forgiven us.

Help us keep our hearts set on you as we navigate through our healing and may we remember the great advice John gives in First

John 2:6: "He who says he abides in Him ought himself also to walk as He walked." Thank You, Father, for giving us the ability to do just that. I pray this in the name of our Savior and Lord Jesus Christ, Amen.

9

He Directs Your Path

Have you ever passed on an opportunity that would've been a great experience for you because you just didn't have peace about it? And if so, did you later wonder if passing it up was a mistake?

My father told me something recently that I still think about when it comes to evaluating or second-guessing what God might be doing in our lives.

My dad is an old-school entrepreneur with an adventurous spirit. He was unafraid of trying new ways of making a living throughout his working years. He prayed about business prospects and knew how to take a hunch from God. He is a social man and through the years he developed friendships which led to getting the inside scoop on opportunities. My dad's reputation for being a man of integrity and his ability to hustle brought many opportunities his way. He had discernment to know when to walk through an open door and when to pass it up.

Recently he was telling me about a time in his life when he had a big job opportunity. It was a career that would've taken him down a different path from where he was headed as a self-employed person. He had reservations about leaving the world of self-employment and chose to decline the job offer. But he had often wondered since then if he had missed the leading of the Lord when he turned down that opportunity. Looking back, he thought that job might have been a better financial choice for his family.

"Yeah, but look at all the things you accomplished!" I told him. "You did well. You always landed on your feet."

His response contained timeless truth: "No Baby, I didn't land on my feet. I landed in the arms of the Lord. The Lord always took care of me. No matter what I did, He was always with me."

That proclamation settled in my spirit and I knew I would never forget that conversation with my dad. His was a simple statement, and a comforting truth. *No matter what I did, He was always with me.* How wonderful to know our Heavenly Father is always with you and me and through it all we can stand because we land in *His* arms first.

God allows us room to grow as we learn to follow Him. Being able to discern His voice is a lifelong journey and we may not always get it right, but He stays with us. I'm a firm believer that if we are prayerfully moving through life, no matter what we choose God will lead us through, He'll bless our efforts, and we'll land where we're supposed to land.

Brandon's Story

Several years ago, my oldest son Brandon, who was living in Tulsa at the time, had just exited an internship program with a Missions organization called Global Ventures. He was blessed to be able to work with Global Ventures for five years. He learned a lot about what it takes to bring the Gospel to those who've never heard the good news of salvation through Christ. He learned about serving, and how to push past the point of comfort to minister to others and get the job done. It was a time of growth in his life as he learned to sacrifice and hone his leadership skills.

The time came when Brandon was ready to exit the program and he was seeking God's direction concerning what to do next. He was working at a local grocery store and had been offered his own store to manage, but he felt that wasn't why he should stay in Tulsa. He believed he had arrived at a crossroads.

One Sunday morning as he sat in a church service, he noticed an employment advertisement on the big screen. It was for a grounds maintenance job at the church. He applied for the job and got it. He loved his new job and really liked the people he worked with. It was an exceptional environment for him and turned out to be the next place God planted Brandon for personal growth.

A New Opportunity

When Christmas time arrived, Brandon came home to California for his yearly visit. One morning we were sitting in our coffee shop talking with a farmer friend about a new crop he was thinking about planting in his farming business. He was looking for someone to bring under his wing and train in the business. After spending the morning with Brandon, he felt like our son would be a good fit for the job and gave him an offer. It was out of the blue, but Brandon felt like it was a great opportunity for a future career, and it would bring him home after seven years of being away.

I remember the day Brandon called with the news that he had decided to move home and accept the job offer. We were excited that our boy was coming home, but almost immediately my heart was uneasy about this change of direction for Brandon. His dad felt the same way; there wasn't a peace about it. We kept the feeling to ourselves and took some time to pray before we talked to our son about rethinking his decision. Our prayer was for Brandon to hear clearly if this wasn't what he was supposed to do, even though he'd already accepted the offer.

Within a day or two, Brandon called us to say that since he accepted the job offer, he didn't have peace about it. He didn't know if it was because he was making the wrong move or if he was just being cautious about leaving the familiar and stepping into a new career. He decided he needed to do some fasting and praying about the move.

At the end of the fast, he still didn't have peace and knew it wasn't the right move for him after all. So, Brandon closed the door on what seemed to be a wonderful opportunity in farming and moved forward with peace in his spirit that he had heard from God. He was satisfied to stay in Tulsa as a groundskeeper for the church. At the time he didn't know why, but he knew God could see what he couldn't. God had a plan for Brandon in Tulsa.

Within one week after making the decision to stay in Tulsa, Brandon got a promotion at his job with the church. He became the supervisor of the grounds crew. Then, after a couple of years serving in that position, he got another promotion to supervisor over the maintenance of church facilities and the grounds as well. Mind you, this church sits on over 300 acres of land and includes a school. This was a big promotion for Brandon. He worked in that new position for a year before being offered *another* promotion – this time to serve as a staff youth pastor. His new position as a youth pastor fulfilled a long-held desire in Brandon's heart to be in full-time ministry. It turned out to be another season in his life in which he grew, learned, and excelled. It was finally plain to see why he experienced no peace about the prospect of moving home to be a farmer. God's plan for him was not to work in the field of agriculture, but in the field of souls.

There are times we are required to simply stand where we are, and wait on God, even if the direction doesn't seem to make sense. The offer Brandon received to work on a farm was a great offer that would have been a place of growth and discovery and greater financial benefit, plus he'd be at home with his family. It made perfect sense and seemed like a no-brainer decision. But God had a different plan, and because Brandon paused and waited on God through fasting and prayer, God directed Brandon's steps to where He ultimately wanted him to be.

In the early years of our marriage, a pastor of ours used to say, "Pray – if you have peace, pursue." I've used that advice a lot. Prayer forces us to pause, and it's in the pause that we can hear the still small voice of God. The check in Brandon's heart about changing course was confirmed when he gave God time to clearly speak.

There is power in the pause. Time can be your friend. If there is an element of uncertainty in a decision, remember to give it a pause. Standing where you are, waiting to hear from God, is never a bad thing. And it's never wasted time. He will lead if you give Him the space in your life to hear His direction.

God Allows the Struggle

I've had my moments of wishing God would just part the clouds and speak with an audible voice. Have you, too, ever wished you could have a clear and audible conversation with God concerning the direction for your life? It can be difficult to hear God concerning major decisions.

The struggle to hear His voice shouldn't be considered a negative. Don't focus on the struggle, itself. Focus on hearing His voice. That focus draws us closer to Him. It requires us to stretch our faith, take a pause, and tune into His frequency.

For Brandon, it wasn't easy. Going in the farming direction made sense in the flesh, but the Spirit required him to resist what made sense in the natural realm and wait on God to speak. He had no idea that staying put as a groundskeeper would eventually lead him to his dream position as a youth pastor.

God doesn't ask us to give up a seemingly good opportunity so He can give us a subpar experience instead. He wants to make our lives impactful and keep us growing spiritually. We just need to trust the process. God will speak, and He will lead. His leading may seem like you're going nowhere at times. Again, waiting isn't easy but eventually you will see how the *leading* of God unfolds the *plan* of God.

Abraham's Servant

I love the story in Genesis about Abraham and his servant, Eliezer.

It's a story about the beauty of being a trustworthy person, about asking God for exactly what you need, having faith for the outcome, and pressing through intimidation to victory. It's a story about honor and faithfulness. It's also a story about God's leading.

Abraham commissioned Eliezer to go to his country and to his family and take a wife for his son, Isaac. God had promised Abraham that the land of Canaan would be given to his descendants, so his daughter-in-law needed to come from his family lineage, from his country.

Eliezer ruled over all that Abraham had. He was Abraham's oldest and most trusted servant and he took this assignment very seriously. Eliezer made an oath to Abraham and asked God for help. He needed God's leading and directions to find the perfect wife for Isaac.

Abraham had assured Eliezer that the Lord would go with him and He would send an angel before him. So, Eliezer gathered some of Abraham's camels and goods and set out for Mesopotamia, the place of Abraham's birth.

When he arrived at a well just outside the city of Mesopotamia, he sat down and prayed this prayer:

"O, Lord God of my master Abraham, please give me success this day, and show kindness to my master Abraham. Behold, here I stand by the well of water, and the daughters of the men of the city are coming out to draw water. Now let it be that the young woman to whom I say 'please let down your pitcher that I may drink' and she says, 'Drink, and I will also give your camel a drink' – let her be the one You have appointed for Your servant Isaac. And by this I will know that You have shown kindness to my master" (Genesis 24:12-14).

Before he was finished speaking along came a woman named Rebekah with her pitcher ready to draw water. Eliezer tested her to see if she was *the one* by asking her for a drink. In her reply, she used the exact words Eliezer had just prayed. God brought Eliezer the confirmation he needed; this woman, Rebekah, was the bride God had chosen for Isaac. Eliezer's prayer had been answered. The story unfolds beautifully in Genesis 24.

It was clear to see that God had blessed every aspect of Eliezer's trip. His mission to find a wife for Isaac was a success and he prayed this closing prayer: "Blessed be the Lord God of my master Abraham, who has not forsaken His mercy and His truth toward my master. As for me, being on the way, the Lord led me to the house of my master's brethren" (Genesis 24:27).

God led Eliezer from the time he made the oath to Abraham to the day he brought Rebekah home to Isaac. I can imagine how relieved and grateful he must have been as he witnessed the approval of Abraham and the joy of Isaac when he took his bride. It was a mission that was perfectly completed.

How God Leads

Just like a bodyguard leads one through a crowd, and protects him or her from surrounding dangers, our Heavenly Father leads us through life and directs our steps.

As I stated earlier, God doesn't audibly speak with daily instructions, nor does He lead with neon signs. He invites us into His presence to seek His direction through prayer as Eliezer did. It is through our moments of quiet reflection and prayer that we can hear God's still small voice leaving impressions on our hearts and depositing truths in our minds.

He leads us through the power of His written Word. We learn His character through His Word which in turn, fosters a common-sense approach when making decisions. He also uses other people to confirm His direction. There have been times in my life when someone spoke a truth that confirmed what I'd been asking God about in prayer. There can be much power in one sentence that is delivered by the Holy Spirit through a friend, pastor, relative, or even a stranger.

God also leads through the preached Word. Just about every

Sunday people tell my husband "that word was for me." God uses the shepherd to speak to the sheep. (That's a great reason for regular church attendance). I've even felt God's leading through the power of music and songs. God knows how to get His message into your ears and heart. He knows how to lead His people.

In my faith experience, I've learned that we all face the possibility – or perhaps even the tendency from time to time – of making a wrong turn. Fortunately, God is bigger than our wrong turns. He's already out ahead of us and has made provisions for those choices. Thankfully, He isn't waiting with a sledgehammer to smack us when we miss the mark. God loves us whether we make the right moves or not. We aren't *always* right but we are always *loved*.

The Ultimate Goal

The most important thing for you and I to remember is that He leads us in the way everlasting.

In John 5:24, Jesus said: "Most assuredly, I say to you, he who hears My word and believes in Him who sent Me has everlasting life, and shall not come into judgment, but has passed from death into everlasting life." And in John 6:47, He reiterated that. "Most assuredly, I say to you, he who believes in Me has everlasting life."

The end goal is heaven, and if you are in Christ, you're going there no matter what your earthly journey looks like. More than likely your life's journey will be full of hills and valleys, twists and turns with some straight-a-ways along the route. Yet, regardless of your struggles and mistakes, as you keep your focus on Him, He will lead you all the way home. What a comforting truth!

Choosing His Path

There have been times I've made wrong decisions in haste and have had to deal with the outcome of those decisions, but I've also learned great lessons from my mistakes. Learning lessons can be a painful process, but God is always so kind to put us back on our feet … after we have landed in His arms.

1. Describe a time when you fell into God's arms before you landed on your feet.

2. What are some things you learned from that experience?

3. Think of someone you know who clearly follows God's lead. What are some of their disciplines or practices that you admire?

4. Do you have any of the same disciplines or attributes? If yes, list them below. If not, what would it take to develop them?

5. List some of the areas of your life in which you recognize God's lead.

6. Is it difficult for you to take a pause in order to hear from God? If so, why do you think you struggle with this kind of pausing?

7. How do the following verses relate to our discussion on pausing?

Psalm 46:10:

Exodus 14:13-14:

Psalm 40:1:

I encourage you to take a notebook to church and write down what you believe God is speaking directly to you from your pastor's sermon in the Word. (This is also a good habit to form as you read your Bible. Pause and ask yourself, *What is God saying in this portion of Scripture that I can apply to my life?*)

God's Desire for You

A great benefit of being a child of God is knowing no matter what, He can lead us to the place He wants us to be. We have a Father who is so good to us. He's given us a perfect roadmap for life. All through the Bible you will see a constant theme, and that is, to simply seek God. He's not hiding from you or me. Scripture says when we seek Him, we find Him (Jeremiah 29:13). When we ask, He answers. May you be encouraged today, and may you find comfort in knowing that the God of Heaven, your Bodyguard, is watching your steps. It is His great desire to lead you to a place of success and peace.

10

He Calms Your Fears

Toward the end of every year my husband asks God for a scripture and a word for our church to focus on for the coming year. I always look forward to hearing the challenge and the inspiration from my husband and Pastor. As we enter into every new year, the goal for us as a church is to keep reaching souls, keep growing, and keep accomplishing Kingdom work. The *first-of-the-year word* has become a tradition for our church, and year after year it has always played out in real time as we watch it come to pass.

It was the second Sunday in 2020, and I sat in the front row listening to my husband preach, wondering what the *word* was going to be for the new year. Some might think because I'm married to the Pastor, I get the inside scoop concerning the upcoming year, but I purposefully don't ask him about that. I enjoy the anticipation.

The words he received from God for 2020 were *fear not*, and the scripture verse was 2 Timothy 1:7: "For God has not given us a spirit of fear, but of power and of love and of a sound mind."

I thought *fear not* was an interesting word since everything seemed to be going well in our country and in the lives of most people I knew. I wondered if God was going to be taking us into new territory as a church, or maybe He would be sending new opportunities to reach souls. Both scenarios would require our faith, not fear. Sometimes in order to move forward in faith we must step over fear, so I began to brace myself and felt some excitement at what the new year would bring.

Never in my wildest imagination would I have thought we'd be bracing ourselves for a *pandemic*.

The year had started out looking promising with a strong economy. The stock market was breaking records, businesses were flourishing, and unemployment numbers were at an all-time low. For the most part, people were thriving and there was optimism in the air that 2020 was going to be a great year. Then came COVID-19.

As I'm writing this chapter the entire country is under a shelter-in-place order. Sadly, the Coronavirus is affecting the systems of the world and taking lives. I've never experienced living through a pandemic and I must agree with the statement I've heard repeatedly: "We are living in strange times."

Fighting an unseen enemy, like a quick-spreading virus, can be very unnerving and cause fear because we don't know what waits for us at the end of it. It's the fear of being sideswiped with the unexpected, the unknown, and the what-ifs. But it doesn't take a pandemic for this kind of fear to creep into our lives. We face other unknowns and challenges that have the potential to create the same kind of fear.

Fear often accompanies times of pain and uncertainty. It also plagues us when we experience events beyond our control. Fear can come after watching someone else go through something we, ourselves, dread. We witness marriages that dissolve, people who struggle with cancer, children who die, and businesses that fail. Fear comes because we've seen first-hand the realities of what these situations can bring. Fear comes because we have a history. We've had experiences that have left a mark on our hearts and our spirits must overcome the silent killer of faith – fear.

Fear is a creeper… it creeps in and attempts to take control of your thought life. Fear is a robber of peace and trust. Fear is the opposite of faith and works in opposition of what faith would do in times of trouble. The Apostle Paul called fear a spirit in 2 Timothy 1:7. You can be sure that God didn't give you a spirit of fear but rather He gave you *His* spirit – one of power, love, and a sound mind. No matter what circumstances exist to cause fear, your unseen Bodyguard stands with you to help you find your way. He's your ever-present Father who loves you and His desire is for you to overcome your fear.

Psalm 119:105 says, "Your word is a lamp unto my feet and a light unto my path." That means His Word lights the steps directly in front of you so that you don't trip and fall. It also means His Word illumines the path ahead, so you can see your way through the dark seasons of life when fear tries to creep in and override your faith. The Word of God is a reassuring agent in our lives, and it brings us peace and truth in the midst of life's struggles. We may not always know what the path ahead entails, but we can know His light is always there to lead us forward.

Overcoming Fear One Ride at a Time

When I was a child my dad built a two-story playhouse in our big country backyard. It was an audacious piece of play equipment. We took the stairs to the top story which had no roof or walls, just a railing all the way around it. It was like a sundeck on top of the roof of the playhouse. I enjoyed being on that rooftop with the strong Schellville winds blowing. I liked spending time there all alone imagining lots of grand adventures, but I stayed away from the sides, due to my fear of heights.

In order to get down from the deck one could take the steps back down or slide down the slide my dad built on the side of the playhouse. The slide was like having a quick escape route when running from my siblings or an imaginary monster. We used to wax the slide to make it a faster ride. That was the fun and safe way down for me. However, there were a couple more options to take for my older siblings. The option my brothers, Mike and Ben, used to take frequently, was jumping from the railing onto a big rubber tube-like thing that was half-filled with air on the lawn below. They called it "the thing." My sister, Gail, used to sit on one end and the boys would jump onto the other end, which would send Gail flying 10 feet in the air (yes, they were wild children and remarkably they never broke a bone).

The last option for getting off the deck was to take a ride down the roller coaster. (Yes, I said rollercoaster.) It was built out of wood and had little wooden carts to sit in. It went from the top of the playhouse, down around the structure, circling the yard to give a bumpy fast ride to the grass below. The rollercoaster had no railings, just a ledge of about two inches on each side to keep the cart from flying off the track. The track was only about two and a half feet wide, requiring the rider to balance herself in the cart before launching from the roof, and hope she didn't lean in one direction too far, or she'd end up on the ground sooner than she should.

My 7-year-old self could in no way entertain the thought of taking a ride on the rollercoaster from the top of the roof. I would watch my siblings fly down with gusto, but it wasn't for me. I was too afraid. It was too high and went too fast. Fear made me a bystander, unable to participate until the day my dad stepped in to modify my ride. He put a cart at the bottom of the rollercoaster, then I'd sit in the cart and he would roll it up the track as far as he could reach, which put me at about seven or eight feet up. Then, he would let go of the cart and I would take a nice safe ride to the bottom. It was perfect for me. As time went by and as my courage grew, I was finally able to take my own trip on the rollercoaster from the top of the playhouse. That became a big day of conquering my fear and ushered in a new era of rollercoaster freedom for me.

It's What Fathers Do

My father wasn't going to allow me to be a bystander and miss the fun of rollercoaster-riding adventures. So, he stood between me and my fear, but He also pushed me to try the ride from a place of safety. In my childlike perception, I wasn't safe because I was closer to the ground (eight feet still felt high to me), I was safe because my father stood between me and the ground, and because he had his hands on my cart. I wasn't going anywhere until he made sure I was ready. His presence calmed every fear I had about taking the ride.

In my years of knowing God, I can tell you today, friend, that no matter how good my earthly father was at protecting, guiding, and loving me, he could never top the love and care of my Heavenly Father. Everything my earthly father knew about my life and what I needed doesn't come close to what my Heavenly Father knows. My earthly father couldn't be a constant presence in my life, and his knowledge was limited to earthly discernment and perspective.

In contrast, my Heavenly Father knew me when I was being formed in my mother's womb (Psalm 139:13). My Heavenly Father breathed life into me, both physically and spiritually. He knows every step I've taken and knows the places I have yet to traverse. He's been with me every day of my life and will continue to walk with me until I draw my last breath.

In Luke 11, Jesus tells us that just as our earthly father knows how to give us good gifts, our Heavenly Father's care is greater. He gives us the Holy Spirit which enables us to live with His power to overcome any fear (verses 11-13).

No matter what challenges you're facing, no matter how afraid you might be today, when you place your life in God's hands, He is a Father who is there for you to give you exactly what you need. He will stand between you and fear. He will hold you in His protective grip and He will lead you. Through the Holy Spirit He will help you overcome the fear of taking on new adventures, no matter how scary or uncertain they may look. God does not expect you to jump into the cart from the top of the roof if you are not ready. But He's also not satisfied to leave you in your state of fear. He doesn't want you to be a bystander while everyone else around you is riding the rollercoaster. He wants you to experience life to the fullest (John 10:10). He wants you to let Him hold you up as high as you can go and then trust Him to release you into your destiny. He wants you to have fun, while you learn to step over fear and move forward in faith. He wants you to be healed from your past, fulfilled in the present, and not fear the future.

Navigating through Fear

Fear can be like storms. One day the sun is shining, and you are basking in its warmth, then overnight the storm front rolls in and changes the whole atmosphere. Events in our lives can be like a storm front that comes in from nowhere to rock our world and cast clouds of doubt and fear.

I think about those who are facing a greater storm than the norm. The winds of their storm are strong, bringing ominous clouds that hold debilitating effects on their lives. Overcoming fear can be a real challenge if you're newly widowed and have never been alone, or you've suddenly lost your job, or you're the parent of a disabled child, or the single mom who was recently diagnosed with cancer. These are heavy burdens and prime opportunities for fear to come in and paralyze.

I have faced my own moments of fear and I've witnessed loved ones walking through unthinkable storms like the ones I just mentioned. Maybe you are facing something similar today. Take heart, friend. No matter how ominous the storm may be, you don't walk alone. You can't see Him, but your Bodyguard is in front of you, beside you, and behind you to help you make it through whatever it is that you're facing today.

When fear begins to haunt you, here is what you can do:

1. Remind yourself of the truth.

You are a child of God and nothing takes you from His hand (Romans 8:39-39). His grip on your life holds you firm and He is bigger than any storm or uncertainty you face. He's the God who commands the wind and the waves and gave the sea its limits

(Proverbs 8:29). He's the God who created the galaxies and gave every star its name (Psalm 147:4). He is your refuge and your strength, and your times are in His hands (Psalm 31:15). He is the God who called you by name, and you are His (Isaiah 43:1). He is the God who defeated fear on the Cross. He is the God who cares about everything that pertains to you (Psalm 139). He sees you and He knows you. His love for you is sure and He will get you through. When you remind yourself of the truth, and declare aloud Who He is and recount His love and goodness, you can stand in faith, not fear.

2. Take inventory of your heart before God.

Get honest with yourself and with Him. Cast your fear upon Him (1Peter 5:7). I do this by quieting my spirit, playing some worship music, and opening God's Word. It is there that faith is mustered, and fear is crushed (Psalm 34:4). It is there at His feet where He speaks peace to my heart and healing to my spirit. Try it and I believe He'll speak to you that way, too. This step is on repeat for victorious living. God doesn't always change your circumstances right away, but He'll cause you to see things with a new perspective and a greater sense of peace (Isaiah 43:2).

3. Remember He is ever-present.

Your God is with you in the best of times and the worst of times. He is continually working for you in ways you can't see. Take comfort in knowing He has a plan for you and for those you love. Be still and know that He is God (Psalm 46:10) and He is working in your life, even when it seems impossible (Psalm 12:7, 77:4; Romans 8:31).

4. Start serving others.

Get busy. Stir yourself up to do some good works, whether it be for the church you attend, for your community, or for a neighbor in need. Ask God to lead you to a place where you can make a difference. Get your calendar out and make some coffee dates or phone calls to people you know who could use a friend or some encouragement or a spiritual boost. Sometimes putting yourself out there externally for others is the best way to conquer what you're going through internally.

Building Faith through the Storm

When talking about overcoming fears and navigating through stormy seasons in life I think of the literal storms in the Bible. God used storms to get people where they needed to be physically, but also to grow them in their faith and to help them overcome their fears.

Let's look at a *fear-and-faith lesson* found in Matthew 14:22-32.

This story took place right after Jesus fed a multitude of people (approximately 10,000-15,000, including women and children). After Jesus and His disciples had a long day ministering to the massive crowd, Jesus commanded His disciples to go to the other side of the sea while He took some solitary time to pray. In the middle of the night, Jesus decided to take a walk across the sea to catch up with His men. The Bible says the wind had become *contrary* and the waves were *tossing* their boat. I can see in my mind's eye, drenched disciples holding on for dear life, being rocked back and forth by the angry waves of the storm. It wasn't uncommon for storms to arise out of nowhere and this was a night when the weather had indeed turned bad. Isn't that similar to what happens to us sometimes? We can be doing fine one day and the next day our circumstances flip upside down. Life can change in an instant. For the disciples, it did. Their journey across the sea started out as a smooth ride, and in a moment everything changed. Can you imagine how fearful Jesus' followers were as they sailed into the center of the storm in the middle of the night?

When they saw Jesus coming toward them, walking on the water, they thought He was a spirit and they were afraid. (I don't blame them. I mean, *who walks on water?*) Immediately upon seeing their fear, Jesus said, "Be of good cheer, it is I, don't be afraid." Peter, being the gutsy one, asked to join Jesus on the water. Jesus was all for it and replied, "Come." And for a few moments Jesus and Peter walked *together* on top of the water!

I love this event in Scripture. For one moment, even though it was just a few steps, Peter and Jesus experienced something together that was absolutely amazing. They defied the laws of nature. Gravity had no hold on them... until Peter's focus was shifted from the Miracle Worker to the elements around him. Scripture tells us when Peter saw the boisterous storm he was afraid and began to sink. As he cried out to Jesus, the Lord reached out and saved Peter from drowning.

I can relate to Peter's moment of fear. He was operating in the supernatural with the sea raging all around him. It was like no other moment in his life. The impossible met up with the natural danger of a raging storm. He had seen Jesus work miracles for others, but this time he was a part of the supernatural work of God! Unfortunately, Peter let the threatening activity of the waves overrule his faith.

There have been times in my life when I've let the circumstances around me affect my peace and bring fear. You probably have, too, but don't feel badly. We see in this story that the disciples did, too, and they lived with Jesus.

After Jesus took Peter's hand and pulled him up to safety, He said to him, "O you of little faith, why did you doubt?" When they got into the boat the storm ceased, and the sea was calmed, and the disciples fell at His feet declaring "Truly You are the Son of God" (verse 33). It was one more confirmation for the disciples as to who Jesus was.

There were a few times in Scripture Jesus had stern words for those close to Him who had a lack of faith, and this night was one of those times. After a day in which they just witnessed the miraculous multiplication of the fish and the loaves you would think there wouldn't be any issues with their faith. Didn't Jesus prove He could do anything? Perhaps that's why Peter requested to walk on the water, he was beginning to get the clue that with Jesus anything is possible.

But then his fear crept in. Remember, fear is a robber of everything that has to do with faith.

I find it interesting that Jesus didn't calm the storm when He set out on His walk. Why not calm the waves early on, knowing that the disciples were trying to get to the other side? He waited to calm the storm until *after* He and Peter got into the boat. Apparently, Jesus wanted to give the disciples and Peter this *faith-over-fear* lesson. While the others looked on, Jesus made Peter face his fear and finish his walk on the stormy water, as if to say "Peter, if you're walking with Me, you have nothing to fear."

Sometimes God allows us to go through the storm to overcome our fears and grow us in our faith as we press through the obstacle to the place of assignment. The disciples and Jesus had an assignment in the city of Gennesaret. God was preparing a time for them there in the city, where many souls would be touched by the power of Jesus. Many people would come from the surrounding regions to encounter the Miracle Worker. It would prove to be a big day of ministering to the crowds. But first they had to conquer the storm. He wants nothing less for you and me. He wants us to be people who know how to persevere to our destiny regardless of what may stand in our way.

My Leap of Faith

Sometimes we miss out on a move of God because we are afraid. Yet, what blessings are waiting for us? What great work is God waiting to release into our lives but doesn't because of the fear that holds us back? The challenge for you and me is to not look at the boisterous elements that surround us which can cause us to fear, or to look at our inabilities that make dreams seem impossible. The goal is to keep our eyes on the One who calms our fears and walks over the top of our storms.

For me, the thought of writing this book, even though it was a long-time desire, brought a certain amount of doubt. I asked both my writing coach and my husband, "who would be interested in anything *I* would have to say?" My argument was "I am an unknown." I was also experiencing an underlying fear of failure. I wondered if I could *finish* a project like writing a book. Would my writing style be compelling enough to hold interest? (You know all the *what ifs* that come into play when considering a new project.) But I had to get my eyes off of what *I* could do and get them back on what *God* could do. I couldn't shake the feeling that God wanted me to stretch myself and take a leap of faith and trust Him with the rest. The outcome of our obedience is up to God. Our part is to simply trust and take the leap.

There is something very satisfying about taking a step, trusting God, and moving forward to conquer your fears. You don't take that journey alone. I know firsthand that He is a God who knows where you're going, and He will be there to calm your fears and lead you into faith.

Resting in the One Who Calms Your Fears

1. What are the fears that keep you stuck on the sidelines? (List them in the space below.)

2. Which of the four steps under Navigating through Fear (on pages 116-117) is the most challenging to you?

How can you begin incorporating that step today?

3. Look up each of the verses of Scripture in the section "Navigating through Fear" and record the ones below that particularly speak to you. Let them lead you to dig into God's Word for more verses that deal with overcoming fear.

4. Think about a time when you had to overcome fear. How did you do it? And what was the outcome? Record it in the space below. (By writing it out, you'll gain confidence from it and you're more likely to remember it.)

Trust Your Father

You may feel like you're in the darkest night, surrounded by fear. Or, maybe you're like me and just trying to overcome a challenge. Whatever the case, God gives you His grace, and having His grace means you have His power to overcome any fear in your life. God doesn't want you to miss anything He has prepared for you, so He stands beside you with your life in His hands, keeping you safe while He pushes you to go as high as you can go. He does this because He not only wants you to grow in your faith, He wants you to have some fun along the way.

Scripture says:

"There is no fear in love; for perfect love casts our fear, because fear involves torment. But he who fears has not been made perfect in love" (1 John 4:18).

Growing in perfect love is a lifelong journey. Let's stay the course…always.

11

He Hears Your
Whispered Prayers

W hen I kissed my husband goodbye on a Friday morning, I had no clue what the day would bring.

Our morning started off as any other. Pete and I had separate agendas for the day, but the plan was to circle around in the evening, as usual, and share dinner together.

After running my errands, and before I returned home, I decided to visit the drive-through car wash. I was in line, sandwiched between two cars when I got *the call* from Pete.

"Hi sweetheart," he said, sounding a bit odd.

"Hi," I replied.

He was out of breath and asked where I was. I told him I was at the carwash, and by the sound of his voice I knew something wasn't right.

"What's wrong?" I asked.

He told me he thought he might be having a reaction to some new diet supplements he'd taken that morning, but wasn't sure and thought maybe I should take him to the doctor. The fact that he didn't think he should drive himself concerned me. I proceeded slowly into the carwash as he described his symptoms.

I told Pete it sounded like he'd had a heart attack. His symptoms didn't fit the perfect heart attack model, but to be safe I thought he should call 9-1-1. We debated that decision as he was already feeling better and didn't think an ambulance was necessary.

We ended our call and I sat there watching the suds drip down my windshield. I thought about whether I should call 9-1-1 anyway. I felt uneasy and decided to call a friend who lived close by to see if he could make a quick visit and assessment.

I took a deep breath. It was unnerving being trapped in the middle of a carwash wondering if Pete truly had a heart attack. I was intending to pray, but instead my mind was bombarded with thoughts. *He didn't sound right. What if this is just a precursor to a major heart attack?*

As my brain continued to conjure up possibilities of what could be happening, I sensed fear creeping in and trying to convince me of the worst-case scenario. I leaned back, closed my eyes, and told myself: *This isn't how I'm doing this; there's no room for fear.* And then I did what I should've done originally. I called upon the One who is always with me. I simply whispered His name aloud – "Jesus." I began to pray in the spirit as I exited the car wash and headed down the road toward home. With every mention of His Name on my lips and every utterance of prayer, peace conquered the fear.

Simple Faith, Simple Whispers

Sometimes, when you and I are faced with uncertainties, all we know to say is His name. At times our need is overwhelming and goes beyond our words and human reasoning. Thank God there is power in that Name. The Name of Jesus.

I'm grateful He hears ours whispers and our unspoken prayers. He hears the sighs in our despair and sees the tears that silently fall. God doesn't need or expect loud, lengthy prayers in order to hear us. In the moments when all you can do is whisper His name, God knows the depth of your need, and sees your faith as you cry out to Him. There can be more faith uttered in a simple whisper, than in an eloquent prayer of many words. Faith is about what's in our hearts, spoken to God in sincerity.

The thief who hung on the cross next to Jesus simply believed that Jesus was who He said He was. His request to the Lord that day as they hung there dying, was a simple one: "Lord, remember me, when You come into Your Kingdom."

Jesus didn't turn to him and deny his request because he didn't' meet certain prayer requirements. Nor did Jesus refuse him for not being a follower of His prior to their crucifixion. No, Jesus knew this criminal was having a moment of revelation and he believed. Jesus responded by saying, "Assuredly, I say to you, today you will be with me in paradise" (Luke 23:42-43). What those words must have meant to the thief as he hung there dying, unworthy of such a gift. I believe the words of Jesus pierced through the darkness and anguish of the thief's soul, and like a mighty wave, peace and comfort must have washed over him, eradicating any feelings of helplessness and doom.

I love this example of a prayer from a desperate soul. This conversation between Jesus and the unnamed criminal shows us how easy it is to receive the free gift of salvation. The love of Jesus was once again on full display as He reached out one last time, to a lost soul, even in His own hour of great distress. Jesus displayed His compassion and His ability to know the heart of every person who cries out to Him, no matter who they are, or what they've done, or where they have come from.

Prayer as a Way of Life

Famed Evangelist Billy Graham was believed to have said that true prayer is a way of life, not just something we use in an emergency. He encouraged us to make prayer a habit so when the need arises we would be in practice.

Having a vibrant prayer life is so important. By *vibrant* I mean giving yourself to prayer on a regular basis. Making prayer part of your daily routine. Not necessarily praying a certain way every day, or for a certain amount of time every day, but simply being with God and being directed by Him in your times of prayer. Jesus instructed

His disciples in Luke 18:1 that they "always ought to pray and not lose heart." He then told a parable in verses 2-7 about the benefits of being persistent in prayer.

Jesus told the story of a widow who sought justice from her adversary by continually pleading her case before an ungodly judge in her city. The judge paid no attention to the woman until he grew tired of her constant pleading for justice. In verse 5 the judge said, "yet because this widow troubles me I will avenge her, lest by her continual coming she weary me." Jesus followed up that story by telling His disciples: "Shall God not avenge His own elect who cry out day and night to Him?" (verse 7). The lesson for the disciples was the importance of persistent prayer.

A vibrant prayer life is a *persistent* prayer life. Sometimes God requires us to persist as we wait and believe.

The Apostle Paul wrote that we should pray always, and he instructed us not to be anxious about anything, but to pray with a thankful heart, making our requests known to the One who can bring peace beyond all understanding (Philippians 4:6-7). Sometimes this passage of Scripture pops into my head when I'm on the go, praying. Let's not forget about the importance of praying always. If Jesus is your friend, you'll talk to Him while you're driving, walking, working in the yard, washing dishes, or sitting still in your "prayer chair." Every prayer doesn't need to be in your private place of prayer, because you don't *live* in isolation. Pray *always*. In your private place for sure, but also as you live your life on the go.

Jesus showed us through His own example what a lifestyle of prayer looks like. He demonstrated by His own life and relationship with His Father that prayer is an essential part of the life of a believer. Consider the importance of prayer in Jesus' life:

- In Matthew 14:23 we read that after a day of ministry, Jesus sent the crowd of people away so He could *go to the mountain* alone and pray.

- In Mark 1:35, Jesus *rose long before the sun* and went to a *solitary place* to pray.
- Luke 5:15-16 tells us as Jesus' ministry began to grow, He often *withdrew Himself into the wilderness* to pray.
- In John 17, Jesus prayed a beautiful prayer of *intercession for His disciples* as the day of His death was approaching.
- And in Matthew 26:39-45, on the night of His betrayal, Jesus went to a garden and *fell on His face before God in prayer in complete surrender* to His Father's will. What He would face that evening and the following day would be horrific and He knew it. So, He prayed like no human has ever prayed. He prayed until his sweat turned into blood. That is some hardcore praying!

After looking at Jesus' life, the importance of regular times of intercession and travailing prayer cannot be overstated. A good prayer life is a balanced, consistent prayer life.

Prayer Prepares

When Jesus rose from that night of intense prayer in the Garden (Matthew 26:46-57), He stood ready to meet His destiny and was prepared to go the distance in a brutal death. He was ready to finish His earthly mission. He looked His accusers in the face and with all the evils of Hell against Him, He humbled Himself unto the Cross. What seemed to his enemies to be defeat, was proven to be total victory as He rose from the grave three days later. What a *powerful* Savior!

I'm always amazed at the power of prayer and what can be accomplished through it. Time spent in prayer adds fuel to faith and helps you know you can conquer whatever lies before you. Prayer brings love to the foreground and helps you see people with a proper perspective. Prayer reminds you of your purpose and drives you into your calling. Spending time in prayer helps you not to sweat the small stuff. Prayer grows character. Prayer positions you to know and hear God, and prayer helps you face your challenges. Prayer changes you. Prayer, whether it's a whisper, or deep intercession, is powerful.

The Rest of the Story

So, what happened to Pete the morning he called me not feeling well? The emergency room doctor said everything looked normal except one enzyme in his blood that showed duress in the heart. To be on the safe side, they ordered him an angiogram. After a long day which included a trip to another hospital for the angiogram (and three stents in two arteries later), we were finally in a hospital room, settling in for the night.

At some point during the evening, my niece Cynthia had joined our party, and was with me as I was leaving the hospital. We gave our goodbye kisses to the patient and Cynthia and I headed for the elevator. We walked and talked about what a long, bizarre day it had been, and before we parted ways, she asked me, "Are you okay? Do you need me to drive you home?" She looked at me intently, almost as if she were examining me and getting ready to judge whether I was going to tell her the truth. *Would she see a hint of an over-stressed Auntie behind an I'm-okay-facade?* It was her job at that moment to make an assessment and to take care of me. I almost felt bad giving her the no-drama answer: "I'm okay." She peered at me for a minute and, convinced that I was truly okay, hugged me and we went our separate ways.

The events of the day hit me as I walked alone toward my car. I knew the day could've ended up with a dramatically different outcome. Tears of gratitude welled up within me and rolled down my cheeks. *Thank you, Father…We're okay because of You.*

Jesus Put the Power in a Whisper

It was a battle of great magnitude the day Jesus faced off against Satan. What Satan thought was the final blow to the Messiah – His murder on the cross – was the plan of God to bring redemption to mankind. The penalty for sin would be remedied once and for all with the shedding of His perfect sinless blood. It was the most powerful day time has ever known. Every slash of the whip He took on his back was for our healing and every drop of blood that fell from His body was for our cleansing (1 Peter 2:21-24; Isaiah 53:3-5). Every sickness, disease, and evil thing was laid upon Him, and He took it all for you and me.

I have no doubt the devil tried to hurl every ounce of his evil power against Jesus as He hung on the cross. I can't imagine going through what Jesus went through on that gruesome day. He was beaten beyond recognition. The whipping He took left gaping wounds, with the flesh and muscle torn from their proper place. In agonizing pain, after carrying a heavy wooden beam on His torn back, Jesus walked up the hill where the hardest part of His journey toward death awaited Him.

Everything would culminate on the cross. The Perfect Savior would be riddled with disease, the Sinless One would take upon Himself the sins of the world, and the effects of the brutal beating from Roman soldiers would render Him weak and wrecked with pain. I imagine the most difficult moment for Jesus came when He sensed an abandonment from His Father who had to look away as He hung dying, taking our sin upon Himself. With nails piercing through His hands and feet and driven into wooden beams, He would hang there feeling forsaken (Matthew 27:46) and alone. For the first time, He was separated from His Holy Father. Certainly, that must have been the most agonizing part of all.

When Jesus declared "It is finished" (John 19:30), death briefly claimed His body, but death could not hold Him. As He promised, Jesus rose from the grave. He rose victorious over sin, sickness and Satan (Revelation 1:16). He did it for *you*. He did it so you could call on His name in your day of trouble. He did it so you could know Him and have fellowship with Him. He did it to secure your future, and to give you His righteousness in place of your sinfulness. He did it to bring reconciliation between you and a Holy God. That Holy God, our Father, now looks at you through the blood of His Son, Jesus. What a powerful act of sacrifice and love from our Savior.

When I ponder all that Jesus did for me on that day of reckoning, there is no wonder why there is such power in the whisper of His name. There is nothing in this life that can stand in the way of His love (Romans 8:38-39). He's already proven that. He is there at the whisper. He is there when we travail. He is there at the shout, the laugh, the sigh, or when silent tears fall. He is *there*.

Cultivating a Life of Prayer

Jesus is with you every moment of every day. In the space below, list some ways you know He's been moving in your life – either outwardly or inwardly, or both. Then thank Him for it.

1. Jesus' victory on the cross secured your victory. Are there areas in your life where you feel like it's a struggle for you to have the victory? Ponder that and write your thoughts below as they come to mind.

2. What do each of these passages of Scripture promise you as you reach for victory? (Write your answer in the space next to each reference):

Psalm 27:13:

John 16:33:

1 Corinthians 15:57-58:

Ephesians 1:

Colossians 1:

1 John 5:4-5:

3. Hannah was a woman who had an aching heart. She lived in a place of barrenness and anguish. Her desperate plea to God was silent at an altar of prayer. Read her story in 1 Samuel 1:2-20 and record in the space below your insights about her prayer:

In light of what you read of Hannah's story, what are you believing God for today?

4. What does Philippians 4:6-7 remind you to do?

Closer than You Realize

Rest assured, friend, Jesus is as close as the whisper of His name. You have an ever-present, all-powerful Father and His love for you has no bounds. He's given you faith and the power of His Name to believe. My prayer for you is that your heart will be stirred to know

Him more and to walk in all that He has provided for you through His Son, Jesus Christ the Lord.

"Blessed be God, who has not turned away my prayer, nor His mercy from me" (Psalm 66:20).

12

He Watches Over You from the Power Seat

Having Pete as my husband is kind of like having a personal bodyguard.

One of the many great attributes he brings to our marriage is his no-nonsense approach to protecting me. He takes his assignment seriously and he lives by the instruction to husbands found in Ephesians 5:25: "Husbands love your wives, just as Christ also loved the church, and gave himself for her." I have never known a time in my marriage when I've felt ignored, unloved, or unprotected. I realize I am a blessed woman because of my husband's obedience to the Word of God.

Whenever we're walking alongside a busy street, I'm reminded of the call on his life to be my protector. He walks on the side next to traffic, and when we're getting ready to cross the street, he always takes my hand and leads the way. I used to get a bit irritated by that and once told him, "Pete, I know how to cross the street." His reply was, "I know you do, but it's my job to protect you." How can one argue with that? So, when we are together, I follow his lead because he is my protector.

The same principle is at work when we go out to eat. When we are seated at the table, Pete always takes the seat that faces the door, or the crowd, so he can see who enters the restaurant and so he can watch the room. If anyone were to enter with dangerous motives, Pete would see it from his seat, and he would act to protect me. We call this the *power seat*. I've had over 40 years to get used to this Ephesians 5:25-kind of living. It has become a way of life for us as a married couple.

Recently our world – and my experience with the power seat – got turned upside down when Pete suffered a terrible accident while cutting a piece of wood on his table saw. The piece of "guide wood" caught on the saw blade and was catapulted into the underside of his forearm. It was a traumatic injury that severed an artery and made spaghetti–like strands out of his nerves. The injury resulted in three surgeries in five days and a condition called Compartment Syndrome.

Pete still has at least one – possibly two – more surgeries after his arm has a year to heal. The surgeon had to fillet his arm on top and on the underside as well in order to make all the repairs. Then it was closed after all the repairs with a "beautiful" skin graft (I say that sarcastically). His arm pretty much looks like a roadmap right now. He wears a covering on it when out in public, so it doesn't scare small children. (Okay that might be an exaggeration, but not by much.) He came close to losing his hand. I'm convinced it was the leading of the Holy Spirit that prevented that from happening.

The accident, and all that resulted from it, was one of the most stressful times in our married life. When the dust settled, I was left feeling weary and a bit blindsided. The year 2020 already had delivered its challenges with the Coronavirus pandemic, shelter-in-place quarantine, racial and political divisiveness, and so on. I really didn't feel like adding this life-altering incident and recovery time to the list of 2020 drama. A friend of mine texted me after the accident and said "sorry to hear you got 2020'd." I thought that was humorous and felt like it would be a good description if I were the superstitious type.

After the accident, not only was my sweetheart unable to protect me, he was unable to do a lot of things during the post-surgery recovery. I was not used to being the one to protect *him* physically. I was not used to seeing him struggle to do everyday tasks and I surely was not used to doing nearly everything for him, like helping him dress, shower, tie his shoes, cut his food, and other seemingly simple tasks. Pete was out of the power seat, and it felt odd.

Faith-Killing Thoughts

One day, while Pete was in the hospital and I was preparing to bring him home, I was praying and feeling vulnerable. I felt the weight of his care and so much more falling on my shoulders. I realize there are a lot of women who are alone without a great man to share life with, and who are raising a family alone. I salute my sisters who are living this reality. I've often said it is the toughest job by far. But, understand that Pete has been my *covering* for 40 years, and this was a new experience for me.

I was fighting sadness – for him and for me. The enemy was attempting to get into my thought life, taunting me with doubts like *What if Pete never gains his strength back in his arm?* and *What if he doesn't regain feeling in his hand?* Satan would whisper things like: *Your life is going to be completely different. A lot of things are going to change now; he's no longer a strong man.* I know it sounds ridiculous, but when we are going through hard times and we are weary and sad, it's easy for the enemy to speak ridiculous thoughts into our spiritual ears. He puts great effort toward filling our thought life with unbelief, fear, and discouragement. His hope is to defeat us and keep us in a pit of despair. The devil likes to kick us while we're down.

As I was praying through these emotions and casting down faith-killing thoughts from the enemy, the Lord reminded me of this truth: God is on His throne. Forever. And because He is also on the throne of my heart, He has complete authority and control over my life.

There is no situation you and I face that has not passed through our Heavenly Father first. Nothing that happens in our lives takes Him by surprise or catches Him off guard.

Our God sits on the ultimate Power Seat. He sees who enters the door of our lives and He is actively watching the room. Does this mean nothing bad will happen? No, that's not what it means. Bad things do happen, and we each have our war stories to prove that. Yet, we are still tempted to ponder the questions:

- *If God is our Bodyguard why do bad things happen?*
- *Where is God when we experience life-altering events?*
- *If God is always watching who comes in the door and all that happens in the room, why do we go through times of suffering and loss in our lives?*

Those are legitimate questions and believe me I've asked God *why* many times in my own life. During times of desperation, I've prayed "God, You said You'd never leave me, and yet I feel alone." Have *you* had those moments when you've wondered where God was during the trying times of your life?

Meeting the God Who Sees

I'm reminded of several people in the Bible who faced heart-wrenching trials and who probably asked the same questions. I think of Hagar, the maidservant of Sarah. Hagar was given to Abraham by his barren wife, Sarai, to bear children since Sarai was unable to. Now before we get upset with Abraham, it's important to note that this type of arrangement was commonly practiced and culturally acceptable in that day. Having children wasn't just a desire in Abraham's day, children were a necessity, especially male children since it was the men of the tribe who provided for the family and protected the family from other warring tribes. For Abraham to have a child whom he could call his heir was crucial. It was also necessary because God promised Abraham that his descendants would be *innumerable* like the stars in the heavens. And because Sarai could not conceive, employing Hagar as a surrogate seemed to Sarai a necessary solution to fulfilling the promise God made to Abraham (Genesis 16:1-4).

But, God didn't need help fulfilling His promise. Sarai's plan wasn't the plan of God and it caused immediate problems between Sarai and Hagar. Sarai ended up despising Hagar. The plan of turning Hagar from "handmaiden" to "surrogate" resulted in jealousy, hatred, and pain.

Hagar was used and rejected by Sarai. The tension between the two women became so unbearable for Hagar that she fled to the wilderness to escape. It was there in the wilderness that she had an encounter with the *God Who Sees*. This moving encounter is found in Genesis 16:7-13:

"Now the Angel of the Lord found her by a spring of water in the wilderness, by the spring on the way to Shur. And He said, "Hagar, Sarai's maid, where have you come from, and where are you going?" She said, "I am fleeing from the presence of my mistress Sarai." The Angel of the Lord said to her, "Return to your mistress and submit yourself under her hand." Then the angel of the Lord said to her, "I will multiply your descendants exceedingly, so that they shall not be counted for multitude." And the Lord said to her "Behold, you are with child, and you shall bear a son. You shall call his name Ishmael because the Lord has heard your affliction. He shall be a wild man; His hand shall be against every man, and every man's hand against him. And he shall dwell in the presence of all his brethren." Then she called the name of the Lord who spoke to her, You Are the God Who Sees; for she said, "Have I also here seen Him who sees me?"

Through no fault of her own Hagar found herself in the wilderness of despair. She was alone and sad. She was doing what she knew to do and that was to leave and rid herself of persecution. Yet, God's command to her was to go back and submit herself to Sarai.

There is such power in submission when it is the last thing you want to do. It's difficult to submit when you've been wronged and treated with disdain. But through her conversation with God she understood there was a *God Who Sees*, and this God was a God who had a plan for her and for her baby, too. God had a purpose for her child and his descendants, as impossible as it may have seemed. All she needed to do was obey His command, go back home, and submit. She had to go back and trust God with her future and that of her child's. Hagar was able to do that because she had heard from the God who saw her in her desperation.

Another Desert Experience

The next time we hear of Hagar, Ishmael her son is a teenager. They had lived and traveled with Abraham as part of his tribe all through the years of Ishmael's young life. When Ishmael was a young teen, the promise of God to Abraham and Sarai (now called Sarah) would finally come to pass. The barren Sarah would conceive and bear a son, the promised heir, Isaac. When that happened, it changed everything.

Once again jealousy came into the household, but this time it was coming from Ishmael. He saw the feast that his father was giving for the toddler Isaac after he passed from babyhood to childhood through the weaning process. Ishmael observed the celebration and the joy of Abraham, and he began to scoff (Genesis 21:8-9). Sarah saw what Ishmael was doing to her son and it enraged her, so she placed another demand upon Abraham, and said "Send the boy and his mother away." Sending them away was not something Abraham wanted to do, but the Lord spoke to him this time and confirmed that what Sarah was requesting was the right thing to do (Genesis 21:10-12). So, Abraham gave Hagar some provisions and sent her and Ishmael away the next morning. Let's pick up the story in Genesis 21:14-21:

"So, Abraham rose early in the morning, and took bread and a skin of water; and putting it on her shoulder, he gave it and the boy to Hagar, and sent her away. Then she departed and wandered in the wilderness of Beersheba. And the water in the skin was used up, and she placed the boy under one of the shrubs. Then she went and sat down across from him at a distance of about a bowshot; for she said to herself, "let me not see the death of the boy." So she sat opposite him, and lifted her voice and wept. And God heard the voice of the lad.

Then the Angel of God called to Hagar out of heaven, and said to her, "What ails you, Hagar? Fear not, for God has heard the voice of the lad where he is. Arise, lift up the lad and hold him with your hand, for I will make him a great nation." Then God opened her eyes, and she saw a well of water. And she went and filled the skin with water and gave the lad a drink. So, God was with the lad; and he grew and dwelt in the wilderness and became an archer. He dwelt in the wilderness of Paran; and his mother took a wife for him from the land of Egypt."

Once again Hagar found herself wandering and desperate in the wilderness. This has always struck me as being a sad story. It must have been devastating to be asked to leave the tribe she had been with for so long, and not only the tribe but the father of her only child and the one who took care of her needs. Her whole world was changed in an instant and I'm sure she was feeling unprotected and vulnerable, once again. And if you look at her circumstance with natural vision that's exactly where she was in her life. Wandering in the wilderness, alone, without water and food, and preparing to lose her life and the life of her son to heat exhaustion and dehydration. I can't imagine what that must have felt like. To leave one's son under a bush to die would be the worst day of a mother's life. And yet God allowed these circumstances. He didn't shield her but rather He allowed her to walk in the desolate wilderness. Wasn't He the *God Who Sees*? Wasn't He the One who made Hagar a promise concerning her son during her first trip to the wilderness? Yes, He was the same God and His promise to Hagar stood firm.

Yet, once again, if God is always with us, why on occasion do our lives get turned upside down? Where is God when those bad things happen to us? If I were Hagar I would have pondered in my heart, *God, I did what You told me to do and went back and submitted myself to Sarah and now this? Didn't You say my descendants would be multiplied? And yet we are here in this wilderness left to die. This isn't multiplication, this feels like elimination!*

Then God spoke from heaven. And Hagar's life completely turned around.

In the moment of Hagar's deepest desperation, God spoke to her and told her He saw her. The *God Who Sees* is also the *God Who Hears*, the *God Who Answers* and the *God Who Provides*. The truth was that no matter how desperate her situation, Hagar wasn't alone, and Ishmael wasn't destined to die. God's plan was about to come into full view for Hagar, beginning with a miracle in the wilderness and a new vision for Hagar. Hagar instantly gained the ability to see an oasis. From that moment, everything in her life changed. That was the place where she and Ishmael settled.

God Always has a Plan

God didn't bring His will to pass for Hagar as long as she stayed under Abraham's covering. Her child wasn't to be Abraham's heir, he was never supposed to be the heir, but yet God still had a plan for him. Sometimes God allows you and me to face struggles and pain to get us where we're supposed to be, so He can accomplish what He has destined for us. As people who are accustomed to comfort, we don't want to believe that God's plan for us could include pain and suffering. But very often it does. Sometimes God's plan for us, like His plan for Hagar, includes some wandering in the wilderness so that we'll become less prideful and more desperate for Him. Sometimes God brings us to the wilderness to remove the scales from our eyes so that we can see clearly His miraculous provision and divine direction. We become completely dependent on God when we are in a place of wilderness. Something beautiful happens in the wilderness if we'll surrender there. We come to know Him as the *God Who Sees*, the *God Who Hears*, the *God Who Answers*, and the *God Who Provides*.

Why do bad things happen if God is watching over you? Bad things happen because we live in a sinful, fallen world. This automatically puts us in the position of having to deal with the downfall or the ruin that came when sin entered the world. Every one of us is challenged to overcome the natural world whether it is sickness, discouragement, pain, accidents, broken relationships, financial stress, and so on. Just by living here on earth we deal with wickedness. If we were living a life free from the sinful fall of man, we would be living in heaven.

He Sees You, Too

Whatever it is that you are suffering through, you belong to God, and He won't leave you. Even though you may not understand your circumstances or why you are going through them, He is still in the power seat and He is still the God who sees right where you are. He hears your cry like He heard Hagar's. And like He did for Hagar, He will make a way in *your* wilderness. He will bring you streams in the deserted places and He will rescue you.

Keep trusting Him, my friend. Keep seeking His will for your life. Keep steady on your journey. That is what I had to do when I was faced with the uncertainties and fears of my husband's injury. I had to keep taking one day at a time with all the added pressure and responsibilities that were placed upon my shoulders. I kept telling myself, *"God sees, God knows, and God gives strength."* My go-to promise in the Word was Romans 8:28 which tells me He works all things together for my good, because I love Him and am called according to His purpose, no matter what.

Whether you are in a season of resting beside the still waters and being refreshed, or if you are wandering, wondering, and waiting in the wilderness, God is with you. He ordains both scenarios in your life. For me, as I finish writing this chapter, I am somewhere in between the two. Life is beginning to resemble some normalcy and yet we are still feeling the brunt of recovering from a trauma. My time through the wilderness isn't completely over, but I'm experiencing some relief and rest as I see God's hand moving during recovery.

As we continue on, my friend, let's remember Hagar. Her time in the wilderness gave way to resting beside an oasis. When Hagar was wandering in the wilderness, she didn't know that God was ultimately going to bring her to a place of refreshing where she would end up settling with her son. God was working in ways she couldn't see. And the same is true for you and me. Even when we can't see it, our Bodyguard is always moving in our lives. Always protecting on our behalf. Always watching the room. And nothing will ever remove Him from the power seat.

Reflecting on Your Desert Wanderings

1. Read Romans 8:35-39. List the various situations that this passage says will never be able to separate you from God's love and presence:

What title does verse 37 give to God's people?

2. What impacts you the most about Hagar's story?

3. According to 2 Timothy 3 what are some of the hardships that Paul had to endure as a Christ-follower?

4. Think about a time in your life when you felt like you were desperate and wandering in a "wilderness."
What was the situation?

How did God bring you out of that place of desperation?

What did you learn through the experience?

In the space below, or in a journal, write a prayer of thanksgiving to God for His faithfulness.

His Presence and Peace Forever

Dear friend, God never promised that we would be free of trials or tribulations. To the contrary, He promised that we *would* experience them. In John 16:33, Jesus said, "These things I have spoken to you, that in Me you may have peace. In the world you will have tribulation; but be of good cheer, I have overcome the world." Thank God He gives us His peace and overcoming power.

In this world everyone suffers; the believer and the unbeliever, alike. The difference for you and me, as believers, is that we can be certain our Heavenly Father is sitting on the ultimate power seat, watching over our lives. Always.

A Parting Encouragement

From the beginning of time until now, God is. As He said to Moses in Exodus 3:14, "I AM WHO I AM." God is all encompassing, all knowing, and ever present. It's difficult to fathom how God can actually be everywhere at all times, but He is. It's hard to imagine that He knows everything about our lives, but He does. He created us exactly the way we are, with all our strengths and weaknesses for His own pleasure, for His glory, and for His purpose. His thoughts toward us are precious and joyful and full of love (Psalm 139:17); these are wonderful facts about God.

You and I cannot begin to understand all the aspects of God or why He does what He does. But you can know about His presence in your life. Just as He made His presence known to me at a very young age, He has been calling you to His side, as well. It's rather remarkable, isn't it? The Almighty, the One whose greatness is unsearchable (Psalm 145:3) bends down and meets with the lowly. He calls us to abide with Him and He invested Himself in our lives when He sent His Son Jesus to take away our sins. I'll never get over that and I hope you won't either.

Although you may not be able to see Him walking alongside you, He is there. His Word attests to it. And His Holy Spirit confirms it.

It's not difficult to recognize the evidence of His presence in our world. Scripture says His works are visible for all to see. The earth testifies to His greatness, the saints tell their stories, and He continues to move in our generation with great signs and wonders.

So, my friend, I guess you really *can* see my Bodyguard.

Let's walk closely beside Him,

Lori

Scriptures to Encourage Your Heart

I enjoy having scriptural references as a quick guide when it comes to dealing with issues of the heart. Here are some of the verses I've referred to throughout this book, plus some others to encourage you and remind you that you are not alone. The God of the Universe always has your back.

God's Comfort:

"You shall increase my greatness, and comfort me on every side" (Psalm 71:21).

"In the multitude of my anxieties within me, your comforts delight my soul" (Psalm 94:19).

"Yea, though I walk through the valley of the shadow of death, I will fear no evil; For You are with me, Your rod and Your staff, they comfort me" (Psalm 23:4).

"Blessed be the Lord God and Father of our Lord Jesus Christ, the Father of mercies and God of all comfort, who comforts us in all our tribulation, that we may be able to comfort those who are in trouble, with the comfort those who are in any trouble, with the comfort with which we ourselves are comforted by God" (2 Corinthians 1:3-4).

God's Protection:

"The Name of the Lord is a strong tower; The righteous run in to it and are safe" (Proverbs 18:10).

"The fear of man brings a snare, but whoever trusts in the Lord shall be safe" (Proverbs 29:25).

"As for God, His way is perfect; The Word of the Lord is proven; He is a shield to all who trust in Him" (Psalm 18:30).

"He shall cover you with His feathers, and under His wings you shall take refuge; His truth shall be your shield and buckler" (Psalm 91:4).

"Hold me up, and I shall be safe, and I shall observe Your statutes continually" (Psalm 119:177).

"The God of my strength, in whom I will trust; my shield and the horn of my salvation, my stronghold and my refuge; My Savior, You save me from violence" (2 Samuel 22:3).

God's Watchful Eye:

"Then she called the name of the Lord who spoke to her, You-Are-The-God-Who-Sees; For she said, "Have I also here seen Him who sees me?" (Genesis 16:13).

"For His eyes are on the ways of man, and He sees all his steps" (Job 34:21).

"The Lord looks from Heaven; He sees all the sons of men" (Psalm 33:13).

"The eyes of the Lord are in every place, keeping watch on the evil and the good" (Proverbs 15:3).

"Lord, what is man, that You take knowledge of him? Or the son of man, that You are mindful of him?" (Psalm 144:3-4).

God's Nearness When You Hurt:

"He heals the brokenhearted and binds up their wounds" (Psalm 147:3).

"In my distress I called upon the Lord and cried out to my God; He heard my voice from His temple, and my cry came before Him, even to His ear" (Psalm 18:6).

"O Lord my God, I cried out to You and You healed me" (Psalm 30:21).

"In the day when I cried out, You answered me, and made me bold with strength in my soul" (Psalm 138:3).

"Heal me, O Lord, and I shall be healed; Save me, and I shall be saved, for You are my praise" (Jeremiah 17:14).

God's Intimate Knowledge of You:

"O Lord, You have searched me and known me. You know my sitting down and my rising up, You understand my thought afar off. You comprehend my path and my laying down. And are acquainted with all my ways. For there is not a word on my tongue, but behold, O Lord, You know it altogether" (Psalm 139:1:1-4).

"But the Lord said to Samuel, "Do not look at his appearance or at his physical stature, because I have refused him. For the Lord does not see as man sees; for man looks at the outward appearance, but the Lord looks at the heart" (1 Samuel 16:7).

"Would God not search this out? For He knows the secrets of the heart" (Psalm 44:21).

"But He knows the way I take; When He has tested me, I shall come forth as gold" (Job 23:10).

"The Lord knows the days of the upright, and their inheritance shall be forever" (Psalm 37:18).

"The steps of a good man are ordered by the Lord, And He delights in his way" (Psalm 37:23).

"Where can I go from Your Spirit? Or where can I flee from Your presence? If I ascend into heaven, You are there; If I take the wings of the morning, and dwell in the uttermost parts of the sea, even there Your hand shall lead me, and Your right hand shall hold me. If I say, "Surely the darkness shall fall on me, even the night shall be light about me; Indeed, the darkness shall not hide from You. But the night shines as the day. The darkness and the light are both alike to You" (Psalm 139:7-12).

"…I am with you always, even to the end of the age" (Matthew 28:20).

God Fights Your Battles:

"The Lord will fight for you, and you shall hold your peace" (Exodus 14:14).

"For the Lord has driven out from before you great and strong nations; but as for you, no one has been able to stand against you to this day. One man of you shall chase a thousand, for the Lord your God is He who fights for you, as he promised you , Therefore take careful heed to yourselves that you love the Lord your God" (Joshua 23:9-11).

"Then all this assembly shall know that the Lord does not save with sword and spear; for the battle is the Lord's, and He will give you into our hands" (1 Samuel 17:47).

God Will Perfect You:

"Being confident of this very thing, that He who has begun a good work in you will complete it until the day of Jesus Christ" (Philippians 1:6).

"And this I pray, that your love may abound still more and more in knowledge and all discernment, that you may approve the things that are excellent, that you may be sincere and without offense till the day of Christ, being filled with the fruits of righteousness which are by Jesus Christ, to the glory and praise of God" (Philippians 1:9-11).

An Invitation to Write

It is my prayer that this book has encouraged you to know Jesus, your personal Bodyguard, in a greater way. If you met Jesus for the first time through this book, or have a story about how He's been there for you or would just like to let me know how this book has encouraged your heart, I'd love to hear from you.

You can email me at loriquerin@sbcglobal.net, correspond with me on my blog at LoriQuerin.com, or drop me a note the old-fashioned way at the address below:

Lori Querin
P.O. Box 653
Kingsburg, CA 93631